D0092666

PUBLIC LIBRARY

ASSAULT ON WEAPONS

Assault on Weapons

The Campaign to Eliminate Your Guns

Alan Gottlieb
&
Dave Workman

MERRIL PRESS
BELLEVUE, WASHINGTON

Assault on Weapons © 2009

Merril Press

All Rights Reserved.

Cover Art Work by Oleg Volk

www.olegvolk.com

No part of this book may be reproduced or transmitted in any form or by any means, graphic, electronic or mechanical, including photocopying, recording, taping, or by any information storage retrieval system, without the written permission from the publisher.

Assault on Weapons is published by

Merril Press, P.O. Box 1682, Bellevue, WA 98009

www.merrilpress.com

Phone: 425-454-7008

Distributed to the book trade by

Midpoint Trade Books, 27 W. 20th Street, New York, N.Y. 10011

www.midpointtradebooks.com

Phone: 212-727-0190

FIRST EDITION

LIBRARY OF CONGRESS CATALOGING-IN-PUBLICATION DATA

GOTTLIEB, ALAN M.
ASSAULT ON WEAPONS : THE CAMPAIGN TO ELIMINATE YOUR GUNS / ALAN GOTTLIEB, DAVE WORKMAN. -- 1ST ED.
    P. CM.
ISBN 978-0-936783-60-4
1. GUN CONTROL--UNITED STATES. 2. FIREARMS--UNITED STATES. 3. FIREARMS--LAW AND LEGISLATION--UNITED STATES. I. WORKMAN, DAVE. II. TITLE.
HV7436.G6755 2009
363.330973--DC22

                                2009027042

PRINTED IN THE UNITED STATES OF AMERICA

DEDICATION

To James Madison, author of the Second Amendment, for his foresight and wisdom in delineating for his fellow Americans and their descendants the one fundamental civil right that separates us from all the other people of the Earth.

With that right comes the responsibility to protect it for all time from those who would erode our liberty and, in so doing, destroy that which has made America the greatest nation in which to raise our hopes, dreams and families.

INTRODUCTION

Citizen disarmament.

It is a term spoken with sincere and deep-seated loathing by American gun owners who have been on one hand energized by the United States Supreme Court's June 26, 2008 ruling in *District of Columbia v Dick Anthony Heller* that affirmed the "individual right" interpretation of the Second Amendment, while on the other hand dismayed and even alarmed that it was a narrow 5-4 ruling that did not mightily strike down all gun control laws, and went so far as to suggest that some gun control is permitted under the Constitution.

Citizen disarmament is how many gun rights activists define gun control, an irrational movement that has been made to sound reasonable, championed by extremists who have been portrayed, and portray themselves, as mainstream Americans. For generations, the gun control movement has promoted various schemes including licensing, registration and gun bans, insisting that each new measure is necessary to make neighborhoods safer, protect children and prevent criminals from getting their hands on guns.

While none of these measures has worked to disarm criminals or stop people from committing suicide or accidentally killing one another, they have accomplished the unspoken goal – the result that all gun control zealots are loathe to acknowledge – of making it increasingly difficult for average citizens to exercise the one constitutional right that sets us apart from citizens of every other nation on the planet: The right to own a gun.

Perhaps due to generations of conditioning depending upon where one grows up, American gun owners have differing perspectives on the right to keep and bear arms that have resulted in division in the ranks. Those who have been raised and still reside in eastern states, where there are registration and licensing requirements, particularly for handguns, have been conditioned through experience to expect these kinds of barriers to gun ownership. Conversely, those who have grown up in the West, where guns are commonly seen in pickup truck window racks, occasionally spotted on the hips of people strolling along rural roads, and suburban and even urban sidewalks, and far more frequently covered by a down vest or denim jacket, view gun control as anathema to all they hold dear.

These cultural divisions within the firearms community have actually enabled the gun control movement to push its agenda, an agenda that dates back more than 150 years and has its roots in racism and social bigotry.

The first gun control laws on American soil were designed to bar freed blacks from arming themselves against post-Civil War night riders who became epitomized by the Ku Klux Klan and glorified in D.W. Griffith's racist *Birth of a Nation*. In the northeast, gun control became a political tool to disarm immigrants – particularly those from southern Europe, and specifically Italy – so that power would be in the hands of bosses such as Big Tim Sullivan and the Tammany Hall crowd of New York City.

But in the Midwest there was gun control as well, via ordinances passed in the famous American cow towns of the 19th Century, under which the carrying of firearms was prohibited in certain areas as a means of keeping the peace. An editor and founder of the *Ford County Globe* newspaper, W.N. Morphy, wrote in a March 5, 1878 editorial that "An honest man attending to his own business doesn't require the constant companionship of a six-shooter to make him feel easy and safe." Morphy added that "there is something rotten with a man's conscience" if he felt it necessary to go armed along the streets of Dodge City.

There it was, an early rendition of an argument that has continued, been refined and updated, that American citizens who are decent, honest and forthright have no need to carry a firearm in public, concealed or otherwise. Only those of questionable character and intent would feel it necessary to pack iron in civilized environs.

For the gun control movement in America, this has become the stereotype and when one cuts through the additional layers of rhetoric, the campaign message against the carrying of firearms really has not changed all that much in the past five generations.

According to a history of early Ford County, Kansas by author Ida Ellen Rath that is available on-line courtesy of the Ford County Historical Society, this Morphy was something of a sickly fellow, recently graduated from law school and suffering from tuberculosis when the newspaper was founded on Christmas Day in 1877. The *Globe* was typical of newspapers of the day, stirring outrage over the presence of gamblers, outlaws and other lowly types and setting them apart as something of a "lower class" from the "decent" citizens.

(Morphy, according to Rath's history, was only around Dodge for a few months before leaving town to head for a more favorable climate for his health. He died, however, about a year later.)

For such "good" citizens, there was the protection of lawmen Wyatt Earp, Ed and Bat Masterson, Charlie Basset and others who enforced the 1877 gun ban north of "The Deadline," which was the railroad tracks running roughly through the middle of town. In 1878, according to other historians, there were only five homicides in Dodge City, and one of those was City Marshal Ed Masterson, shot dead by a drunken cowboy named Jack Wagner, whom Masterson had apparently thought he disarmed moments before. Masterson returned fire, mortally sounding Wagner, who died the following day.

That killing took place on April 9, slightly more than a month after Morphy's editorial appeared. Masterson's death served to reinforce the notions promoted in the *Globe*.

Times have changed, but the rhetoric from gun control proponents has remained remarkably similar over the span of more than 130 years: There is no place in a civilized society for an armed citizen; honest people do not need guns for personal safety; only those of low moral purpose would feel the need to go armed.

Anti-gun editorialists rarely miss the opportunity to use the death of a peace officer to promote their anti-gun ownership philosophy, and so it was even in the aftermath of Masterson's slaying. On April 13, 1878, the *Dodge City Times* observed, "He died in the service he performed so well, and has added one other to the list of those who, living, were so many representatives, each of his day and generation, but who dead, belong to all time, and whose voices ring down the ages in solemn protest against the reign of violence and blood."

Compare Morphy's arguments with those put forth by gun rights opponents in today's America. In 2006, Kansas State Sen. Phil Journey, a former member of the National Rifle Association's Board of Directors and a veteran Kansas gun rights activist, pushed concealed carry legislation through the Legislature,

The effort allowed an anti-gun forum called "The Gun Guys" to editorialize, "Dodge City didn't want concealed weapons in the 1870s because they realized that concealed weapons are nothing but dangerous. They don't stop crime, they don't protect the populace, and they're nothing but a costly threat to citizens. They had the sense to get rid of them, and if Kansas' lawmakers have half of their sense, they'll keep concealed weapons out of Dodge City and everywhere else in the Sunflower State for another hundred years."

Likewise, the Brady Campaign to Prevent Gun Violence, the most active gun control advocacy in the nation, insists, "There should be strict limits on public carrying of concealed handguns. If CCW permits are going to be issued, law enforcement should have broad discretion to issue or deny CCW permits based on what is best for public safety. In states that allow for law enforcement discretion, most police agencies are more cautious about whom they allow to carry concealed handguns in public."

When concealed carry reform legislation was being debated in state after state during the 1990s, gun rights opponents – the same people who insisted the Second Amendment was never intended to protect a fundamental, individual civil right to own a gun before the 2008 Supreme Court ruling, and since have complained that the high court was wrong – actively lobbied in state legislatures, arguing that such right-to-carry statutes would lead to more violence, increase the threat to police officers, lead to more shootings by juveniles and allow private citizens to engage in gunfights at traffic accidents, stop lights and in bars and taverns.

Gun control has become a political issue perhaps equaled only by abortion in its bitter divisiveness. It is something of a political litmus test, with Liberal Democrats supporting gun regulations that range anywhere in severity from inconvenient to extreme, and conservative Republicans and Libertarians opposing restrictive measures on the grounds that they violate state and federal constitutional protections, and are an affront to liberty and personal responsibility.

Over the years, Democrats became known as the "party of gun control" because as the party drifted incrementally farther to the Left, controlling guns by demonizing the people who owned them became something of a mantra. Despite documented political losses to the party at the state and federal levels over the gun control issue, even in 2008, the party retained gun control as part of its national platform.

After the District of Columbia lost its historic case before the Supreme Court, ending more than a quarter-century of handgun prohibition in the city, its liberal Democrat administration continued to wage a campaign of discouragement designed to keep district residents from exercising their recently-restored right to keep a handgun in their own homes for personal protection. In order for citizens to legally keep handguns in their homes, they would have to go through a registration process, the gun would be examined, and the firearm would have to be kept locked and unloaded until it was actually used for self-defense under rules thrown together in the wake of the court decision.

City leaders could call it anything they wanted, but in the final analysis the regulations were specifically written to discourage as many District residents as possible from arming themselves.

Likewise, licensing and registration have been used in New York under the Sullivan Law for a century to discourage average citizens from having firearms. In New York City, it takes months for an average citizen to be given the okay to obtain a handgun license, and there is no plausible explanation for such a lengthy process. In Illinois, gun owners must possess a Firearm Owner Identification (FOID) card in order to legally own a firearm.

Legislation has been passed to ban certain types of firearms or severely limit their ownership and possession at state and federal levels. The National Firearms Act of 1934 was the first such piece of federal legislation, imposing an excise tax on machine guns and placing severe restrictions on their possession, in reaction to gangland violence in the late 1920s and early 1930s. The Act categorized certain weapons which had previously been legal to possess, and put them in a special class that included not only machine guns but short-barreled rifles and shotguns, suppressors ("silencers") and a curious category called "Any Other Weapon," the most prominent of which was the (at the time) rather popular Harrington & Richardson "Handi-Gun," a pistol chambered for the .410 shotshell that had a barrel length of either 8 or 12.25 inches and was used for small game hunting.

In 1939, the Supreme Court handed down a confusing ruling in the case of *U.S. v Miller,* which has been deliberately misrepresented, as much as simply misunderstood over the years. Gun control advocates used a somewhat strained interpretation of that ruling to presume, and insist through years of legal arguments and interviews, that the Second Amendment protected only a collective right of the states. That was hardly true, since the Miller court actually only ruled that a sawed-off shotgun could not be considered the kind of weapon that would normally be used in militia service. The *Miller* case was decided, however, with only one side of the case being argued before the court. Neither the defendant in that case, nor his legal counsel, were present. Only the government argued its side of the case.

In 1968, Congress passed the Gun Control Act in reaction to the assassinations of the Rev. Dr. Martin Luther King and Sen. Robert F. Kennedy. That federal law banned the importation of firearms classified under the earlier 1934 law, dubbing those guns "NFA weapons." It halted mail-order sales of rifles and shotguns and added further restrictions on legal gun ownership, none of which, critics have argued, resulted in any measurable reduction in crime. Indeed, there are some contentions that the so-called "GCA '68" actually contributed to the expansion of an illegal "black market" gun trade.

Four years after passage of the 1968 law, enforcement authority was assigned to the Department of the Treasury, which expanded its Alcohol and Tobacco tax division to include firearms, thus creating the Bureau of Alcohol, Tobacco and Firearms (BATF) in 1972. Almost from the outset, the BATF earned a reputation for over-zealousness to the point that Michigan Congressman John Dingell in 1981 blistered the agency's conduct by referring to BATF as "a jackbooted group of fascists."

The District of Columbia handgun ban was adopted in 1976, and a virtual ban on handguns in Chicago, Illinois began in early 1982. Subsequently, a handful of Chicago suburbs (Morton Grove, Oak Park,

Winetka and Wilmette) banned handgun possession, Morton Grove's ban becoming the most famous of the lot for the publicity it received and the fact that a court challenge failed.

In 1994, the Democrat-controlled Congress passed a law banning, for a ten-year period, manufacture and sale of certain types of military-look alike semiautomatic rifles, though it did not ban the sale or possession of existing guns already in private hands. By the time the ban expired in September 2004, experts were at the very least divided as to its effectiveness in reducing violent crime. Yet gun control proponents worked feverishly to pressure Congress to renew the ban, expand its scope and make it permanent essentially acknowledging that the ban was more symbolism than substance, in that it represented the first time a class of firearms had been subject to a nationwide ban. The gun control lobby did not wish to lose this trophy legislation.

The next serious focus of anti-gun attention became the rather large and cumbersome genre of rifles designed to fire the .50 BMG-caliber cartridge. Demonizing this family of rifles was easy because they appear menacing to people unfamiliar with firearms, and rhetoric against these guns was over the top almost from the beginning. They were labeled "long-range terrorist rifles" and, without any challenge from an all-too-complacent and gullible media, the gun ban advocates were able to cultivate the outright myth that these rifles could be used to shoot down commercial jetliners.

When guns are not directly being targeted, firearms dealers and gun shows are subjected to the same kind of demonization. Dealers have found themselves portrayed as scurvy characters who illegally peddle guns out the back door to criminals. Gun shows have been called "arms bazaars" for criminals and terrorists, despite ample evidence that such a claim is utter nonsense. A study done for the Department of Justice revealed that less than 1 percent of prison inmates convicted of violent felonies got their guns from gun shows.

On the horizon may come a major legislative effort against so-called "sniper rifles," which might be defined as any centerfire rifle equipped with a telescopic sight that is capable of being fitted with a bipod and that fires a projectile capable of penetrating police bullet resistant vests. All of this amounts to fraud, because such rifles are used by big game hunters all over the country, and it is well-known that common hunting bullets will go through soft police vests, which are designed to stop *handgun* bullets.

Gun owners strenuously fought a proposed ban on so-called "armor-piercing bullets" some years ago because of the very fact that such a ban would outlaw every bullet used in every centerfire hunting rifle in America, and the gun control lobby knew it.

What such bans are truly all about, according to several leading gun rights advocates, is that they "condition" the public to the notion that banning certain firearms is acceptable. Ultimately, through the piecemeal process, these gun rights activists have warned, bans would be gradually expanded to encompass a broader number and types of firearms until one day the public will be virtually disarmed.

One can classify such an argument under "conspiracy theory" if one is so inclined, but the true pattern of gun control is that it has slowly expanded, adding layers of bureaucratic red tape and incrementally restricting the type of firearms and the manner of carry or even storage. The gun control lobby has been skillful in pushing laws that it has later called "weak" while demanding additional laws with even more restrictions. They have adopted buzzwords such as "modest," "reasonable" and "sensible" to disguise the insidious nature of such statutes, all of which are ultimately designed to reduce the number of citizens who may own firearms, either by "disqualifying" them via legal technicality or through sheer inconvenience.

We have arrived at a point in our national history that leaves both sides of the gun control debate temporarily stymied. The Supreme Court has affirmed that the Second Amendment protects an individual civil right to own a gun, yet has left intact a maze of local, state and federal gun control laws that have in many ways gutted this single great liberty. Gun control advocates are not happy because there now stands a barrier to their dream of one day eradicating firearms from society. Gun ownership activists are perhaps slightly less unhappy, but hardly delighted, because there still stand many barriers to the exercise of a fundamental right that seems to have been stipulated in our Bill of Rights as a means of protecting all of our other rights.

We are not at an impasse, and this is hardly a checkmate, because the doorway through which the Second Amendment must pass to its next phase of interpretation – whether it is limited or may be expanded to render moot many of the onerous statutes now on the books –

swings both directions. There remain legal battles aplenty to determine whether laws that might regulate the exercise of Second Amendment rights face strict scrutiny or some lesser degree of scrutiny. It must also be determined whether the Second Amendment can be incorporated to affect the states and place limits on state legislatures as it does on Congress.

The fact that such battles remain to be waged is proof positive that the campaign to eliminate gun ownership is far from over, and the issue is entirely unsettled.

So long as there are radical organizations such as the Brady Center to Prevent Gun Violence, the Violence Policy Center and their network of state affiliates calling themselves "CeaseFire" organizations, which work with sympathetic anti-gun politicians, the relentless campaign to abolish private gun ownership in the United States, and crush the constitutional amendment that protects this right will continue.

CHAPTER 1

A Philosophy of Hatred and Fear

'I hate guns!"

It is a matter-of-fact expression that one hears all-too-frequently from people who have become activists in the anti-gun movement. There is no arguing the point, no sense in attempting to find a reasonable middle ground; people who are driven to the extreme position of not simply disliking firearms but wanting to ban them.

The late Col. Jeff Cooper, an internationally-known firearms trainer, writer and philosopher called such people "hoplophobes" and suggested that they suffer from what he called "hoplophobia." He defined this affliction as "a mental disturbance characterized by irrational aversion to weapons."

Cooper first used the term in 1962, but today there is actually clinical acceptance that such a phobia exists, as acknowledged in *Contemporary Diagnosis And Management of Anxiety Disorders*, a 2006 book authored by Doctors Phillip T. Ninan and Broadie W. Dunlop, available on Amazon.com.

These people to whom Cooper alluded to disdainfully as hoplophobes quite often do not explain this abhorrence toward firearms, as many of these adamant gun haters all-too-frequently have no cogent explanation, as in having had some horrible personal experience. When they do discuss this aversion, their remarks are typically steeped in hysteria, and they will use horrific, isolated examples of violence, such as school shootings, and speak of these acts as though they were commonplace.

Epitomizing this vehemence, writer Sallie Tisdale wrote in a *Salon* column, "Why must we listen to the claims of gun lovers, or make any effort at all to satisfy their irrational appetite for weapons? Why should we bow to the rage and hunger of a single-issue lobby? Why should we think for even one more second that freedom means the freedom to own terrifying weapons of mass destruction?"

A few sentences later, Tisdale came clean: "I am no longer an advocate of gun control. I am an advocate of gun elimination."

While there has probably always been some apprehension toward firearms among some people, the hysteria toward guns and gun owners is a relatively recent phenomenon in an historical sense, arising over the past 40 years since the assassinations of John F. and Robert F. Kennedy and Dr. Martin Luther King, coinciding with the eruption of the anti-war movement that opposed the war in Vietnam.

The gun control movement has become a powerful albeit small and vocal lobby – powerful particularly when sympathetic liberal Democrats command majorities on Capitol Hill and in the state legislatures, and because they are well-funded by the Hollywood elite and billionaires like George Soros. This lobby has friends throughout the print and broadcast media; reporters who are accustomed to using inflammatory terms such as "high-powered assault weapon" in their crime coverage, editorial writers who argue strenuously against gun ownership, and for increasingly restrictive gun control statutes, cartoonists who consistently portray gun owners as rather loathsome people with pot bellies, low foreheads, and stupid facial expressions, and copy editors who cannot seem to be technically accurate, thus the stories they allow to be published are frequently misleading.

Of course, over the past 40 years, there has been much violent crime in American society; too much and it is perpetrated increasingly by inner city youth gangs, members of which are not even old enough to legally own firearms, and many who are in this country illegally. Many of these young thugs are already recidivist criminals with histories of arrest for various crimes, yet they are repeatedly shown leniency by the courts. The quickness of such youthful criminals to resort to lethal violence over some miniscule slight is alarming, and it may be reflective of a generation raised in homes where the father was never present to teach by example the notion of personal responsibility. After all, some sociologists might argue, how does one teach responsibility by example when one has been so irresponsible to father a child and then disappear entirely from the life of the child and its mother?

It becomes no stretch of logic to understand how an increasingly urban and suburban populace having little or no practical experience with firearms could come to fear guns. In their environment, guns are nearly always linked to some criminal act that leaves only physical and emotional pain in its wake. Thus, people tend to be wary if not downright fearful of anyone with a gun, because guns are associated with crime, and lawful gun owners are stereotyped as contemporary Neanderthals who care nothing about neighborhood safety, and everything about their right to cradle a loaded firearm; the beer-swilling, overweight, under-educated sloth who beats his wife and starves their children.

It does the firearms community no good when individual gun owners deliberately go out of their way to promote the stereotype, whether brandishing a highly accessorized semi-automatic rifle in a YouTube video, or appearing at a public meeting in soiled, rumpled clothing with a three-day beard growth to oppose some gun control measure, while using provocative language.

For the hoplophobe, all of these elements combine to provide a foundation for this fear and loathing of firearms and the people who have them. For them, the stereotype becomes the reality; gun owners are a sub-class of individuals considered less intelligent and more prone to less-than-intellectual solutions for any problems they encounter. They accept the caricature of a gun owner as an accurate portrayal, perhaps to further justify their aversion to firearms, and thus the social bigotry they feel toward armed citizens.

Exploiting this scenario, gun control lobbying organizations have emerged to further the philosophy of citizen disarmament, primarily through legislation and occasionally through the courts. While they call themselves by progressive-sounding titles, such as the Brady Campaign to Prevent Gun Violence (formerly Handgun Control, Inc.), the Violence Policy Center or the Coalition Against Gun Violence, their campaigns are not nearly as focused on preventing criminal violence as they are on outlawing as many guns as possible, and finding ways to either discourage or prevent as many Americans as possible from legally owning firearms.

Writers like Tisdale cooperate in pushing the hysteria with remarks such as this from her *Salon* article: "Imagine your worst nightmare, your scariest neighbor, your angriest employee or the most frightening student at your child's high school loading up on ammo this weekend at a convention center near you. It's perfectly legal. It happens all the time, and we act as though there is nothing we can do about it."

Yet Tisdale's remarks might pale in comparison to the hysterics most often issued by the Brady Campaign and its president, Paul Helmke. The Brady Campaign's approach to any legislation that expands or simply protects the rights of American firearm owners is typically a "sky-is-falling" reaction.

For example, after the United States Supreme Court ruled on June 26, 2008 that the Second Amendment affirmed and protected an individual right to keep and bear arms, the District of Columbia was left to deal with a handgun ban that had been struck down as unconstitutional. The city, in an attempt to circumvent the high court ruling as much as possible, and make it prohibitively difficult for District residents to keep loaded handguns in their homes for personal protection, adopted an interim ordinance that continued to prohibit the ownership of semiautomatic pistols, and only allowed citizens to register revolvers. The ordinance further required that guns be kept locked with trigger locks until they were used for self-defense purposes, which was clearly and knowingly in direct contradiction to the Supreme Court ruling. That ruling not only struck down the handgun ban, but it also declared unconstitutional a provision that firearms be rendered inoperable by various means, including the use of trigger locks.

Finally, the U.S. House of Representatives entertained (and ultimately adopted) a statute that stripped firearms regulation from the authority of the District council.

Reaction from the Brady Campaign's Helmke was predictably hysterical and alarmist.

"This legislation will endanger public safety in a city that is already a target for terrorists," he declared in a press release. "It will allow dangerous people to stockpile dangerous weapons and it will make it harder for the people of D.C. to combat gun violence in their community."

Before he concluded, Helmke capitalized on the opportunity to press the Brady Campaign's long-standing agenda against gun shows.

"Instead of allowing the gun lobby to weaken gun laws in our Nation's Capital," he lamented, "Congress should be strengthening our woefully inadequate Federal gun laws by requiring background checks for all gun sales, including at gun shows; closing the gap that gives known or suspected terrorists an opening to buy guns; and giving law enforcement more tools to fight illegal gun trafficking."

Research conducted for the Justice Department has demonstrated, however, that gun shows are the source of less than one-percent of the guns used by armed criminals. Helmke knows this. Presumably so do reporters and their editors, but rarely does anyone allude to this in print.

As a result of these acts of omission, the public is left with the impression that gun shows are safe havens for every manner of thug and lunatic, and that firearms flow freely in and out of such places. The stereotype is perpetuated, and the myth becomes the reality.

It would be understandable, one presumes, to firearms owners if anti-gun activists would approach the subject honestly and simply acknowledge that they dislike firearms. There has been no loud demand from the firearms community that all citizens should be required to own and carry weapons. The preposterous nature of such a notion has never been lost on gun rights activists who have historically maintained that nobody should be required to own and carry a gun if they object to it, but by the same token, no citizen should be deprived of the right to do so if they so choose.

Invariably, it has been the anti-gun movement that has insisted society operate as a reflection of its values. Gun owners as a whole have maintained a rather benign outlook, contending that they would much rather be left alone to enjoy their own pursuits rather than be engaged in a constant battle defending their lifestyle choices.

This dilemma seems to be resurrected every few months and most often when it coincides with elections. It can certainly be exemplified by people like author Tisdale, quoted earlier in this chapter, who admitted up front in her *Salon* essay that "I've long been an advocate of gun control, long frustrated by the craven attitude of many legislators when faced with the gun lobby."

She begins by stating her position, and then declares that lawmakers who fundamentally disagree with her reasoning are toadies to gun rights organizations. She is essentially stating that "If you don't agree with me, you are scum and your ideas have no merit."

Tisdale did not stop there. She went on to criticize the suggestion of Donald Kaul, who had written in the *Chicago Tribune* that a solution to the debate over gun ownership might be "a compromise that balanced the needs and desires of gun enthusiasts with the need of society to protect itself..."

But Tisdale – easily reflecting the rigid philosophy of the obstinate gun control movement – quickly demanded to know "Why do we need to balance the 'needs and desires of gun enthusiasts' with anything at all?"

Such rhetoric is unfortunately typical of adamant gun control advocates, for whom there will never been any contentment until firearms, and perhaps their owners, are eradicated from society. Tisdale loaded her column with alarmist rhetoric like "gun lovers" and "terrifying weapons of mass destruction" designed to unnerve readers into believing that typical gun owners are unbalanced to the point of doting over firearms which can be unleashed at any second to cause massive death tolls.

This willful distortion has served the gun control lobby very well over the past couple of generations, not merely criticizing guns and their owners, but demonizing them. Author Workman has occasionally noted that gun owners are the only segment of the population against which is it still considered acceptable, perhaps even stylish, to practice social bigotry.

This hatred and fear has manifested itself in many ways. For example, gun ban proponents have fostered efforts to persuade parents to call their neighbors and ask if there are any guns in the home before they allow their children to go play with their friends. One might reasonably argue how politically incorrect it would be if a parent were to call the parent of her child's playmate to ask "Are there any blacks or gays in your house?"

Yet asking if there are firearms in a home would seem to be a gross invasion of privacy that is hardly limited to just neighbors asking one another about their possessions. In the medical community over the past several years, it has become acceptable, even commonplace, for physicians to ask new patients whether they own any guns, and then to provide gun safety tips. There are several problems with this, not the least of which is that it is what a group calling itself Doctors for Responsible Gun Ownership (DRGO) calls a "boundary violation." That is, a physician asks a question that has nothing to do with treatment of a disease, so it is outside the boundary of necessary medical information.

Here's the official DRGO definition: "A boundary violation takes place when a physician breaches the patient's trust and uses his authority to advance a political agenda."

Doctors are trained and licensed to practice medicine, and unless they are certified firearms safety instructors, they have absolutely no business offering gun safety advice to patients. It would be the same as a layman advising someone on how to treat cancer or set a broken bone, or actually stitching up a wound.

However, for several years, activist physicians who also happened to be gun control advocates, used the color of their profession, and steered the American Medical Association, to promote gun control as a public health issue, and gun ownership as a public health menace. They developed patient questionnaires that sought information about firearms in the home, and they lobbied hospitals to ban firearms including those carried by legally-licensed private citizens.

Such actions by anti-gun physicians and writings by gun control proponents such as Tisdale demonstrate the insidious nature of a social prejudice. It is the prejudice, not the ownership of firearms that has become the true menace, because it quickly escapes rationality, and becomes – as Cooper noted earlier in this chapter – "a mental disturbance characterized by irrational aversion to weapons." Like a disease left untreated, this bigotry spreads.

This "hoplophobia" of Cooper's description is probably not curable like any genuine disease, because it is a problem rooted in emotion and philosophy, rather than anything physical for which one might develop a serum. One simply does not take two aspirins and wake up in the morning sans his or her unreasonable fear of firearms with which they took slumber the night before.

The reason one cannot shake this impulse to hate or fear firearms is because writers like Tisdale perpetuate those fears and hatreds with remarks like her: "Imagine your worst nightmare…" quoted earlier.

Yes, Tisdale and people of her socio-political persuasion want others to be afraid, for it is that fear which she and other gun prohibitionists seek to exploit in their effort to abolish firearms from the landscape, as though such a feat would be remotely possible. At the time Tisdale wrote her column, which can still be found on the Internet, she lamented that there were in the neighborhood of 200 million firearms in the United States, 35 million of those having been manufactured during the previous ten years.

"They've been added to our daily lives, to our shopping malls, neighborhoods, city parks, street corners and schools," Tisdale warned, as if there is a firearm lurking behind every park bench or shrub, waiting to leap out and enthrall some passerby like a dancing cobra. "According to the Coalition to Stop Gun Violence there is now a gun for every single adult in this country and for every other child. A new handgun is made in this country every 20 seconds."

The Coalition to Stop Gun Violence is hardly a monument to impartiality, in a far more aggressive way than the National Rifle Association is an admitted partisan advocate for its cause of promoting and defending the Second Amendment. The vast difference between the two groups is that the NRA has been around more than a hundred years longer than the Coalition, and has far more members who come from all walks of life and background. While the Coalition and similar groups work tirelessly to impose their philosophy on all of society, the average NRA member is quite content to be merely left alone to live his or her life as they see fit.

Besides, it can be demonstrably argued that even with so many millions of guns pouring into society, firearm accident rates have been falling, and in many areas of high per capita gun ownership, crime rates are declining.

Another critic of gun ownership whose hysteria pandering is as dependable as the sunrise is Josh Horwitz, executive director of the Coalition to Stop Gun Violence. In a February 2008 column appearing on the far Left liberal *Huffington Post,* Horwitz verbally sneered at the notion the U.S. Supreme Court might rule – as it did just four months later – that the Second Amendment "protects an individual right to possess arms to defend against the 'depredations of a tyrannical government'."

Demonstrating either a complete ignorance or deliberate misrepresentation of historical fact, Horwitz dismissed this fundamental purpose of an armed citizenry – one that can be confirmed historically – as an "insurrectionist viewpoint" fostered by the NRA.

"This insurrectionist philosophy has long been embraced by proponents of the view that the Second Amendment protects an individual right to possess firearms unrelated to service in a government regulated militia," Horwitz wrote condescendingly.

One might argue that Horwitz and his colleagues had been living in a communal state of denial prior to the high court's ruling in the landmark case of *District of Columbia v. Dick Anthony Heller,* the celebrated Second Amendment case that struck down a handgun ban in the nation's capital. For years they had insisted that the "right of the people to keep and bear arms" was narrowly related to service in a militia, a supposition they had endeavored to press into the nation's constitutional framework, and thus into the national consciousness.

When the Supreme Court ruling, written by Justice Antonin Scalia, was release, the wails of anguish emitted by gun control advocates, declaring an end to civilization as we know it, revealed just how extreme their beliefs were in relation to the opinion of the court and the majority of Americans, who have repeatedly told polls that they overwhelmingly accepted the Second Amendment as protective of an individual civil right.

Joining Horwitz in this radical departure from the mainstream, the "Gun Guys" forum – a deliberately misnamed Internet website devoted to gun control – decried the individual rights definition of the Second Amendment. Reacting to Horwitz' column, the Gun Guys wrote, "are we going to condone militia style organizations who believe that the government is 'oppressing them,' and that they have a right to engage in an armed rebellion? Can we afford to give unregulated firearms access of military grade weapons to people who believe that black helicopters are hovering over them and monitoring their every movement and thought?"

Here, again, the gun control lobby plants the not-so-subtle suggestion that those who believe in an individual right to keep and bear arms, and who understand this right in its true historical content, are nuts in tinfoil hats worrying about government mind control. This is their carefully manufactured caricature of the typical gun owner, a raving looney who hears voices at night and listens for the whirling beat of black helicopter rotor blades over his house. It is yet another manifestation of the on-going campaign of social bigotry against firearms owners. If one cannot demonize gun owners, one stereotypes them as crazy people in need of counseling if not outright institutionalization, and if the public subscribes to this stereotype, soon the image becomes the reality and there follows a consensus that such people certainly should not be allowed to have guns.

It is a campaign whose existence is borne out by indicators ranging from the ridiculous to the sublime. The term "gun nuts" is a prime example, one that is casually dismissed by the very gun control proponents who habitually use it to refer to anyone who owns a firearm and believes he or she has that right. The term is both condescending and derogatory, and meant to be. Branding someone a "gun nut" automatically categorizes that individual as intellectually inferior and perhaps not well balanced emotionally. An anti-gun newspaper columnist can call a group of gun rights activists "gun nuts" and when someone protests the label, the columnist can then dismiss the anger as the ranting of an "over-sensitive gun nut."

Perhaps the best example of this sneering social bigotry, or the worst depending upon one's perspective, came in 2008 with the debate over changing national park rules to allow the carrying of licensed, concealed handguns for personal protection. Nowhere in the rule would there be allowances for target shooting or hunting, or any kind of casual discharge of a firearm.

This did not prevent opponents of the plan to suggest otherwise in an effort to sway public sentiment. Anti-gunner Josh Sugarmann, writing on *The Huffington Post*, quoted a letter sent to the U.S. Senate by the Association of National Park Rangers, U.S. Park Rangers Lodge of the Fraternal Order of Police, and the Coalition of National Park Service Retirees. In their letter, these groups asserted that "wildlife will not remain easily viewable when it is being shot at."

The rule change would not allow shooting at animals, and these organizations knew it.

The letter also stated, "…many rangers can recite stories about incidents where the risk to other visitors--as well as to the ranger--

would have been exacerbated if a gun had been readily-accessible. This amendment would compromise the safe atmosphere that is valued by Americans and expected by international tourists traveling to the United States."

Pure supposition, substituted as fact, but that did not prevent these groups from demonizing armed citizens by suggesting that they might endanger others simply by being present in the area.

The ranger groups further argued, "This amendment could hamper efforts by park rangers to halt poaching, a chronic problem in many national park units throughout the country… because possession and display of a weapon would no longer be probable cause to initiate a search for evidence of wildlife or wildlife parts."

These groups knew that the rule change would apply strictly to *concealed handguns*, not hunting rifles or shotguns, muzzleloaders or bows and arrows, all the tools of poachers. Yet they endeavored to perpetuate the notion that handgun-carrying citizens would be shooting wildlife.

The Brady Campaign's Paul Helmke chimed in with the rhetorical question, "Why are we putting hikers, campers and families at risk by introducing loaded, hidden handguns into our national parks and refuges?"

Again, the mere presence of a firearm, in Helmke's view, is a danger to everyone else in the vicinity, regardless whether anyone even knows it is there. Were this fear related to any other issue, the press might regard it as unwarranted paranoia.

And then the *Salt Lake Tribune* remarked, "…the rule will ruin the experience for many guests who, unaccustomed to the open display of firearms, encounter gun-toting hikers on the trail.

"Wildlife will also suffer. Poaching, according to the National Park Service, has contributed to the decline of 29 wildlife species in the parks. In 2006, 406 incidents were reported despite the firearms ban.

"Now, with visitors free to carry guns, impulse and opportunistic killing of wildlife, along with firearms-related vandalism, will increase dramatically. Professional poachers, who sell animal parts on the black market, will operate with near impunity. And armed visitors will be more likely to approach animals, resulting in unnecessary confrontations and the needless destruction of wildlife."

Here, again, the newspaper editorial writers told readers something that is verifiably not true. The original rule applied to the *concealed* carry of firearms, not open carry. They portray armed citizens as random, spontaneous killers of park wildlife, when there is no data to support that stereotype.

Gun control activists are loathe to admit that gun owners, or gun rights organizations, can ever do anything right that produces a benefit to society. It is rare enough that examples can be hard to find, but in an April 2000 column appearing in *Philadelphia's City Paper*, writer Noel Weyrich found himself extolling the benefits of a tough-on-crime program championed by the NRA. The article was headlined "What if the Gun Nuts are Right?"

Weyrich began his column asking, "Could locking up bad guys save more lives than gun control? The success of Operation Cease Fire suggests the answer is yes."

The piece told the story of one recidivist drug dealer in Philadelphia, and how he ended up in a federal penitentiary when he might have otherwise anticipated a proverbial slap on the wrist. The NRA had teamed up with federal prosecutors to start hitting armed criminals with a legal sledge hammer. As a result, Weyrich noted, violent gun-related crime had taken almost 150 of the city's worst repeat offenders off the streets for extended prison stays.

After studying the success of this program, Weyrich wrote: "With their history of fanatical opposition to even the simplest of gun-control measures, the NRA and its Pennsylvania affiliates have long been political pariahs in Philadelphia, a city that has been bleeding to death for decades from drug-related warfare. Many local police, in particular, despise the NRA for its insane opposition to a federal ban on Teflon-coated 'cop-killer' bullets — bullets designed for the express purpose of piercing police body armor.

"Yet with Exile and Cease Fire," he continued, "it is quite possible that the NRA has already helped prevent more gun violence in Richmond and Philadelphia than any gun-control law ever has.

"True, the NRA may be a bunch of gun nuts," Weyrich added, still unable to resist stereotyping NRA members. "But when the NRA claims that controlling criminals makes a lot more sense than controlling guns, the Cease Fire experience in Philadelphia suggests that on this single point, the gun nuts may be right."

One supposes that praise is good from whatever the source, and however it is begrudgingly couched, but Weyrich's remarks reflect the reluctance to say anything positive about a firearms organization without descending to the attack level. Essentially, he is giving credit to the "gun nuts" for accomplishing something, while reminding his readers, "but they're still nuts."

This approach coalesces with efforts by anti-gun medical professionals to classify violent crime involving firearms as a public health menace. By so doing, these pro-gun-control physicians reinforce the proposition that firearms owners are somehow equal to carriers of a plague. Thus, one might presume if one carries this notion to a logical conclusion, it is in the public interest that such people be identified, their rights restricted or heavily regulated, and that the virus they carry – the virus being firearms – be eradicated.

Doctors Against Handgun Injury urged in its newsletter to physicians that they sign petitions supporting legislation that would ban so-called "assault weapons." This newsletter also advised recipients that, "DAHI has put together kits that will provide physicians and other health professionals with helpful materials on gun injury prevention. The kit includes brochures for physicians and patients, fact sheets, and policy information."

These "kits" constitute the sort of "boundary violation" that was alluded to earlier. DRGO President Dr. Timothy Wheeler has fought such violations as exceeding the scope and authority of what medical practitioners should be doing in the examination room. But the kits, and the reasoning behind them, are yet another manifestation of the social prejudice against guns and their owners, and it lends credibility to the practice of this type of bigotry.

Other physicians, particularly those who are gun owners, are fighting back, however. Dr. Miguel A. Faria Jr., editor in chief of the *Medical Sentinel*, the official journal of the Association of American Physicians and Surgeons and author of *Vandals at the Gates of Medicine* and *Medical Warrior: Fighting Corporate Socialized Medicine*, took the medical profession – his professional colleagues – to task for their effort to find out whether their patients own firearms.

"With this new incursion into gun politics by the medical profession," he wrote in the *Medical Sentinel*, "it's easy to see why patients may be more reluctant and less candid than ever with their physicians, which may, in turn, be detrimental to their medical care."

Faria, Wheeler and others were alarmed at the time that Dr. Richard Corlin, an activist anti-gun physician had ascended to the presidency of the American Medical Association. In his inauguration speech before the AMA, Corlin told physicians, "(Gun violence) is a battle that we cannot *not* take on. People have told me that this is a dangerous path to follow. That I am crazy to do it. That I am putting our organization in jeopardy. They say we'll lose members."

Dr. Faria, in his commentary, fired back: "Dr. Corlin has put his own personal agenda and self-aggrandizement at the expense of all physicians and the AMA, the organization that claims to represent all of us."

Whether it is physicians fighting back against efforts to politicize their professional organization, or firearms owners battling the practice of social bigotry, perhaps AMA's Corlin was right: This *is* a battle we cannot *not* take on.

If we have come so far as a society to reject bigotry in all of its ugly forms, then there should be no place for the kind of emotional and social segregation gun control extremism would have us adopt toward gun owners. Now that the Supreme Court has affirmed gun ownership is a fundamental civil right, efforts to stigmatize the exercise of that right can no longer be casually condoned, much less encouraged.

An attack on one civil right that is rooted in hatred and fear is a threat to all civil rights, and those who fail to see this, or simply ignore it are enabling those who perpetuate it.

CHAPTER 2

'Nobody Needs an AK-47'

Perhaps the late John Hosford, a retired sheriff's deputy who served with the King County, Washington sheriff's department and later became the executive director of a gun rights organization in Washington State called the Citizens Committee for the Right to Keep and Bear Arms, put it best.

"The day they tell me I can't have an AK-47 is the day I'm probably going to need it."

Hosford was at one of his most philosophical moments when he made that statement years ago, before he retired and moved to Wyoming after having served a number of years at the Bellevue, WA-based organization.

He was, perhaps, reacting to early efforts to ban so-called "assault weapons." Having suffered a gunshot wound in the line of duty, Hosford was a formidable opponent to anyone who claimed police officers uniformly support all manner of gun control.

One might also suggest that Hosford could see over the horizon and understood that the effort to ban semi-automatic look-alike versions of popular military rifles would use as a cornerstone argument, "You don't need one of these to hunt deer." Even in those days, some 20 years ago, Hosford was quick to retort that "the Second Amendment is not about deer hunting."

True enough, the "You don't need an...." argument has permeated the extremist gun control lexicon in various forms for a generation. The dialogue occasionally has alterations, depending upon the season and venue, to include "for duck hunting" or "for deer hunting."

Gun rights leaders have countered that "It's not a Bill of Needs, but a Bill of Rights." No citizen needs to justify his or her exercise of a fundamental civil right, and when the debate begins shifting to whether one needs this or that gun to shoot deer or ducks, seasoned gun rights activists will note that one does not need a Ferrari or even a Ford Mustang merely to drive from home to work, or from one city to another, either. If someone does not need a rifle that can fire more than ten rounds out of a single magazine, one could hardly need a car designed to travel faster than the posted legal speed limit.

During the 2008 presidential campaign, when Illinois Sen. Barack Obama made his acceptance speech at the Democratic nominating convention in Denver, Colorado, he pontificated, "The reality of gun ownership may be different for hunters in rural Ohio than for those plagued by gang-violence in Cleveland, but don't tell me we can't uphold the Second Amendment while keeping AK-47s out of the hands of criminals."

The authors, in an opinion piece that ran in several newspapers at the time, responded that, "The 'reality' is that gun rights are the same for everyone, no matter where they live." American gun owners know from experience that Democrats falsely believe that the only way to keep guns away from criminals is to oppressively regulate gun ownership for everyone, a subject explored in more detail in *These Dogs Don't Hunt: The Democrats' War on Guns*, an earlier effort by the authors.

That book traced the anti-gun history of the Democrat party, from the post-Civil War South and politically corrupt New York City of the Tammany Hall era, to today's environment of liberal political correctness.

Whether gun control proponents will ever acknowledge it, the fact remains that in order to keep firearms out of the hands of criminals, their only strategy is to disarm everyone, and if history has taught this nation one thing it is that no law will ever prevent criminals from getting their hands on guns. The ten-year ban on so-called "assault weapons" that expired in September 2004 was allowed to die not because of pressure from the National Rifle Association and other gun rights organizations, but because Congressional lawmakers were able to look over ten years of data and it revealed that there had been no measurable impact on violent crime as a result of the ban.

The law didn't work, and it had created nothing but infringements on the rights of law-abiding firearms owners, so it was allowed to expire off the books.

But this ban is a significant symbol to the gun control movement. Gun control activists, who invented the term "assault weapon" as it applies to semi-auto firearms and quickly gulled an all-too-cooperative liberal press into repeating the term *ad nauseum* – often preceded by "high-powered" to further enhance the demon image to such guns – still wants its trophy legislation revived.

In reality, these rifles are not the "high-powered" menaces that anti-gunners claim they are. The AK-series of rifles and carbines, used the world over by military units and insurgent terrorist groups, fires a cartridge, the 7.62x39mm, that is powerful enough to kill a deer — and, indeed, has become a popular deer hunting cartridge in the upper Midwest — while the American AR-15 and its clones fires a cartridge that was originally developed to shoot varmints, small game and coyotes. In many states, this cartridge, the 5.56mm NATO (or .223 Remington), is illegal for hunting deer and elk because the bullet it too small and it lacks penetration and stopping power, while in other states such as Wisconsin, the AK-type rifle with its .30-caliber cartridge, is very popular among hunters who cannot afford a more expensive hunting rifle.

While AK-type rifles and carbines have grown popular among budget-minded deer hunters, what these rifles are exceedingly good for is predator control, home defense and informal competition. They are remarkably versatile utility rifles, well-suited to these purposes, and they are owned by millions of American citizens who have never entertained the slightest notion of violating the law.

The problem that firearms prohibitionists have with such rifles is not so much their power as their appearance, and it is this appearance that the gun control lobby has been able to exploit. The AR-15, with its black synthetic stock, pistol grip, long magazine, high profile front and rear sights and flash suppressor at the muzzle simply look menacing to people not familiar with firearms. Anti-gunners have been successful in their efforts to confuse the public into thinking such rifles are machine guns, when that is simply not true. In actual operation, they are essentially no different than a 75-year-old Browning shotgun or the little .22-caliber semiautomatic rifle many youngsters use when they are learning to shoot. For each shot, the shooter must deliberately press the trigger. None of theses firearms discharge more than one round at a time unless they seriously malfunction.

But as retired sociology professor William R. Tonso noted in his superb essay '*Unspeak*' and the Gun Prohibitionists that appeared on LewRockwell.com, gun control extremists capitalized on the public confusion to press for the ten-year "ban" on these firearms passed during the first Clinton Administration.

Tonso recalled in his essay: "In his 1988 'report on assault weapons,' gun prohibitionist Josh Sugarmann wrote: 'The weapon's menacing looks, coupled with the public's confusion over fully automatic machine guns versus semi-automatic assault weapons – anything that looks like a machine gun is assumed to be a machine gun – can only increase the chance of public support for restrictions on these weapons. In addition, few people can envision a practical use for these guns.' In other words, Sugarmann expected public support for a ban on 'semi-automatic assault weapons,' because that public was completely uninformed about the guns so labeled. And he expected the public to stay uninformed about these guns, because, as he candidly acknowledged, the media the public looks to for information were equally uninformed about them. In fact, the mainstream media often encouraged the public to believe that the semi-automatics targeted by the prohibitionists were actually machine guns, the legal civilian possession of which has been strictly regulated by the federal government since 1934 and which is not allowed at all by some states. For five years after the 1989 Stockton, California schoolyard shooting, in which such a gun was used, every NBC and many CNN commentaries on 'assault weapons' that I viewed that included demonstrations, showed machine guns rather than the semi-automatic guns covered by the eventually-passed ban being fired. And these machine-gun demonstrations were invariably accompanied by snide comments by either the TV anchor or a guest ban supporter to the effect that such guns were obviously of no use to hunters, often referred to as 'sportsmen.' Never mind that the guns being demonstrated weren't the guns covered by the ban, or that opposition to the ban had nothing to do with the desires or needs of hunters, or that legitimate gun use isn't limited to hunting."

People were further confused about such guns thanks in no small part to action television series like *Miami Vice* in the early 1980s.

Paul Helmke, president of the Brady Campaign to Prevent Gun Violence, perpetuates the hysteria by frequently alluding to these firearms as "military-style semi-automatic assault weapons." This deliberate demonization of a class of firearms that are functionally identical to the Browning shotgun grandpa used for duck hunting has been effective in convincing many Americans that all such firearms should be banned. It does not occur to those with little or no working knowledge of firearms that by supporting such bans they are essentially criminalizing grandpa and his fine old shotgun.

Getting such firearms banned may be more difficult now that the Supreme Court has ruled that outright bans on specific types of guns does not pass constitutional muster, but it is not entirely outside the realm of possibility.

However, the "next best" measure in the opinion of gun control proponents is to classify all such firearms as machine guns, thus regulating their ownership in the same way that private ownership of fully-automatic machine guns has been regulated in the United States since 1934. Owners would be required to obtain special licenses and jump through other regulatory hoops.

Can anyone imagine their grandfather having to be fingerprinted, and have his background checked, and be assessed $300 simply to continue owning that weathered old Browning semiautomatic shotgun? Can anyone imagine grandpa being arrested for having such a firearm without a license?

While gun control proponents and the politicians who follow their siren's song repeatedly insist that they are not going to outlaw guns, when that is precisely their agenda, one firearm at a time.

It does gun owners no good when one of their own literally steps into the limelight, attempting a political statement that only reinforces the stereotype of a "gun nut." Witness the Democratic presidential primary debate of July 2007 in which a Michigan man held up a highly accessorized AR-15 rifle and told a national audience that the gun was his "baby." This demonstration, regardless how well-intentioned, allowed perennial anti-gun Democrat Sen. Joe Biden to remark "he needs help," as if the citizen with his rifle were mentally unstable.

"I don't know that he is mentally qualified to own that gun," Biden remarked.

The other public relations hurdle to be overcome by gun rights activists is the fact that, like it or not, several mass shooters in recent times have been armed with such rifles, particularly the AK-style firearm. It was the gun used by Chai Vang, a 36-year-old Hmong immigrant living in Minnesota to shoot eight Wisconsin deer hunters in a dispute over the use of a tree stand on private property in November 2004.

The same type of firearm was used by 19-year-old killer Robert A. Hawkins in the Westroad Mall rampage in December 2007 in Omaha, Nebraska.

Colorado gunman Matthew Murray was armed with at least five firearms including two handguns when he showed up at the New Life Center in Colorado Springs, within a few days of the Omaha shooting in December 2007. He had hundreds of rounds of ammunition and had left a note declaring his intention to kill as many people as possible.

However, gun rights activists can properly argue that it was a private citizen licensed to carry concealed that stopped Murray literally in his tracks before he was able to open fire on the church congregation. Jeanne Assam shot Murray several times before he reportedly took his own life.

Helmke, meanwhile, and other gun control lobbyists have also convinced a large segment of the public that criminals have "easy access" to firearms. Indeed, the "easy access" argument is thrown into much of their rhetoric, with the predictable reaction from the public being support for additional restrictions on law-abiding citizens.

Those gun-owning and gun-buying citizens have a far more difficult time getting guns today than they did 25 years ago. Criminals have always had access to firearms, because they do not obey the law or follow the legal requirements for purchasing guns.

The National Instant Check System is one hoop through which law-abiding gun buyers must leap, and if there is any kind of waiting period, that also must be obeyed. If there is a one-gun-per-month purchase restriction, that's another roadblock.

People like Helmke would have the public believe that no such restrictions apply, yet the Brady Law — named for Jim Brady, the man wounded in the 1981 assassination attempt on President Ronald Reagan — requires the background check and Helmke knows it. The "easy access" rhetoric is one more tactic in the effort to bamboozle people into believing that anyone can simply stroll into a gun shop or a gun show and purchase any kind of firearm they want, no questions asked.

It makes no difference that the firearms affected by the 1994 Clinton ban on so-called "assault weapons" were found to have been used in less than 2 percent of all crimes involving firearms according to a study for the National Institute of Justice. The NIJ study noted that data compiled from 38 different sources produced the 2 percent average on crime gun involvement. That study was done by researchers Christopher S. Koper, Daniel J. Woods and Jeffrey A. Roth at the Jerry Lee Center of Criminology, University of Pennsylvania and released in June 2004 under the title *An Updated Assessment of the Federal Assault Weapons Ban: Impacts on Gun Markets and Gun Violence, 1994-2003.*

In summarizing their findings, the authors noted, "The gun ban provision targets a relatively small number of weapons based on outward features or accessories *that have little to do with the weapons' operation* (emphasis added). Removing some or all of these features is sufficient to make the weapons legal. In other respects (e.g., type of firing mechanism, ammunition fired, and the ability to accept a detachable magazine), [assault weapons] do not differ from other legal semiautomatic weapons."

This has never mattered to gun prohibitionists. The major objections to private widespread ownership of semiautomatic sport utility rifles are largely grounded in fear of the gun's cosmetics rather than actual involvement in crime.

Ironically, the 1994 Clinton ban — which many, including former President Bill Clinton, believe led to a political bloodbath that year when gun owners descended on the polls and threw out more than 50 Democrats who voted for the measure, including then-Speaker of the House, Rep. Tom Foley of Washington State — was not a true ban, but was largely "cosmetic" in its own right. The ban merely halted production of specific firearms with specific features and limited their magazine capacity to ten cartridges.

The ban did not prevent gun manufacturers from altering the appearance of their gun models by removing the visually offensive features, such as bayonet lugs and flash suppressors (which have nothing to do with the operation of the firearm) and continuing to sell those altered guns. Likewise, the ban did not prevent the sale of pre-existing full-capacity magazines that carry 20 or more cartridges.

Nor did the ban outlaw these guns. It was still legal to own them, and even sell them, they just could no longer be manufactured and had to be sold with ten-round magazines.

Yet even with the continued availability of semiautomatic military look-alikes, crime rates involving such firearms declined.

When the ban was allowed to expire in September 1994, gun ban advocates hysterically declared to a seemingly gullible press corps that there would be anarchy and blood in the streets. Their doomsday scenario never materialized.

When they are not endeavoring to demonize so-called "assault weapons," those who oppose the individual civil right to own firearms spend much of their energy attacking another target, the family of cumbersome rifles chambered for the .50 BMG cartridge. These 19-26 pound rifles, developed for long-range recreational shooting (at such targets as water-filled plastic garbage cans, empty oil drums, buckets and other oddball objects) have been dubbed "sniper rifles" by the gun ban lobby because they were adapted for military purposes several years ago. Naturally, many in the press quickly adopted that term and use it repeatedly in their writing.

Because they really are visually intimidating to the non-shooting public, these rifles — whether they are single-shot models, bolt-action repeaters or semiautomatics — are easy to criticize, and moreover, have become the subject of horror story myths. The most popular of these blatant prevarications is the notion that a shot from one of these rifles would be capable of bringing down a commercial jet. Aircraft experts would counter such nonsense by recalling how, during WWII, military bombers such as the B-17 and B-29 were frequently shot full of holes by German fighter pilots or seriously damaged by German flak, and those aircraft managed to fly hundreds of miles back to their bases in England.

Even the most capable marksman would have a difficult time at best hitting a fully speeding aircraft during takeoff or in low flight with one of these rifles. These aircraft are traveling at speeds ranging to 500-600 plus miles per hour in flight, and even during takeoff, they are speeding down the runway at between 150 and 180 mph. It would take the ultimate degree of skill, coupled with no small amount of sheer luck for a terrorist using one of these rifles to hit a commercial jet and damage it enough to bring it down.

All of today's commercial jets have dual systems; that is, they have "back-up" systems in the event something fails.

But to further dismiss the hysteria surrounding the .50-caliber rifle, one need only recall the incident involving Aloha Airlines Flight 243 on April 28, 1988. The flight left Hilo Airport bound for Honolulu and during the flight, the plane — a Boeing 737 — lost an 18-*foot* section of the fuselage that included both roof and sides. One flight attendant was lost when the roof blew away, and several passengers were severely injured, but the plane made an emergency landing at Maui's Kahului Airport.

Contrast that with a half-inch hole that would be made in the unlikely event that a plane was actually hit by a round fired from a .50 BMG-caliber target rifle. It is doubtful the plane would even lose much cabin pressure.

Much the same nonsense was pandered in the months following the Sept. 11, 2001 terrorist attacks when the Citizens Committee for the Right to Keep and Bear Arms spearheaded a movement to arm commercial airline pilots against any subsequent skyjacking attempts. Anti-gunners, and even some government officials who were cool to the idea—which quickly garnered support from airline pilots and travelers' groups—and argued that a pistol bullet fired through the plane's fuselage could cause quick decompression and a crash, as depicted in the 1964 James Bond film *Goldfinger.*

At the time, a Boeing spokeswoman assured author Workman that the movie depiction was pure Hollywood hokum, and added that cabin pressure would quickly stabilize. A story about this appeared in *Gun Week.*

This revelation has not stopped the alarmist rhetoric, of course. The Brady Campaign has long promoted public paranoia over .50 BMG rifles, when there may be but a single documented criminal use of such a gun on American soil, in an armored car robbery some years ago. If these guns were linked to a crime epidemic, it would be national news.

But here's how the Brady Campaign portrays the .50-caliber rifle: "Capable of destroying armored personnel carriers, aircraft and bulk fuel and ammunition sites, the .50 caliber sniper rifle is now proliferating in the civilian market. Accurate at up to 2,000 yards (20 football fields end-to-end) it can inflict effective damage to targets over four miles away. With more power on impact then any other semi-automatic rifle legally available on the civilian market, the .50 caliber represents a serious threat to our local law enforcement and national security."

These rather awkward and expensive rifles (prices range upwards to about $3,500 - $4,500, depending upon model and accessories) certainly can hit *stationary* targets at 2,000 yards, but a moving target is questionable. Bullets fired from these rifles can penetrate hard armor, as demonstrated in the first Gulf War, and there are some special projectiles available for the military that cannot be owned by civilians.

While the .50 caliber rifle represents one thing publicly in the view of the Brady Campaign and similarly-minded gun prohibitionist organizations, it quietly represents something else: A trophy.

The 1994 ban on certain semiautomatic firearms was a trophy statute to the gun control lobby, and the feverish battle they waged to preserve it demonstrated just how much a ban meant to them. They also vigorously defended the handgun ban in Washington, D.C. that was struck down by the landmark ruling in *District of Columbia v. Dick Anthony Heller* in June 2008.

The reason for such zealous defense of a handgun ban is not because they believe that removing a specific type of firearm from the public arena will reduce crime. That's nonsense and even the anti-gun lobby realizes it. The real rationale behind pursuing and defending gun bans is far more insidious.

If the gun control lobby can convince people to initially support such a ban, this creates the impression in the public consciousness that a firearms ban of some sort is perfectly acceptable. Thus, if you can lobby hard enough to ban one type of firearm today, it becomes a little easier to come back tomorrow and campaign for a ban on some other type of firearm tomorrow.

By labeling the .50-caliber model a "long range sniper rifle," and convincing a state legislature or Congress to enact a ban on private ownership of such a gun, perhaps next year, a more typical centerfire hunting rifle with a black synthetic stock, bipod and high-power telescopic sight will become the new demon gun. Such rifles are far more common, yet a skilled marksman can consistently hit very small targets out to several hundred yards with one of these rifles.

These "all-weather" rifles – in common calibers such as the .30-06 or .308 Winchester – are built specifically for big game hunting, primarily in damp or rugged environments. The synthetic stocks are impervious to weather, which makes them popular among hunters in the Pacific Northwest, Alaska and the Northeast. Barrels of stainless steel further enhance the capability of such guns to withstand the elements.

In the eyes of an extremist anti-gun activist, however, this might be the weapon of the anti-Christ, particularly if the Violence Policy Center's Sugarmann were to fabricate some sinister stereotype of the gun based solely on its appearance. If the gun control lobby were to launch a campaign against such rifles, that would certainly be how they would be portrayed, the "portable sniper rifle."

What would happen with such a ban, or at least some type of licensing and/or registration requirement? Virtually every big game hunting rifle in the country and literally all varmint rifles fitted with riflescopes would fall within the definition of "sniper rifle."

The more likely scenario, of course, would be a push to severely limit the availability of handguns. Recall that the original name of the Brady Campaign to Prevent Gun Violence was Handgun Control, Inc. This organization may have changed its name but it has never changed its core philosophy, which explains its defense of the handgun ban in the District of Columbia and the anguish over its demise on Second Amendment grounds.

The organization, and its various clones, revealed early on the fear that striking down the District gun ban would lead to legal challenges against similar bans in Chicago and that city's suburbs. Of course, that is what happened. Several small communities around Chicago repealed their handgun bans and almost immediately after the Supreme Court ruling in *Heller*, Chicago was sued by the Second

Amendment Foundation, Illinois State Rifle Association and National Rifle Association.

What is significant among the various gun control groups is that they simply do not accept the high court ruling in the *Heller* case. They cling to the argument that the Second Amendment never was intended to protect a fundamental individual civil right, and because the ruling was a narrow 5-4 victory for the gun rights community, it is possible that the gun control lobby believes it may one day overturn the *Heller* decision.

That would require a philosophical shift on the Supreme Court, and that could only be made possible by the appointment of liberal justices by a liberal president, acting in concert with a Democrat-controlled Congress.

That would be a long-range goal, and certainly not out of character for a powerful lobby that has been waging a decades-long battle to incrementally erode the rights of American firearms owners. Erosion is a slow, deliberate process and gun owners are certainly in the fight for the proverbial "long haul."

The most immediate goal of this erosion process is to demonize and ultimately eliminate semiautomatic rifles and shotguns from the landscape, which brings us back around to the contention that "you don't need an AK-47." This argument has always had a fundamentally flawed subtext, as gun rights activists can respond with the far more substantial contention that nobody has appointed the Brady Campaign or Violence Policy Center to be the governing body of what citizens "need" and conversely what they "don't need." It is quite evident that these anti-gunners have appointed themselves to be making such decisions.

The attitude of gun prohibitionists is "Why shouldn't we have the prerogative to make such decisions?" It is this philosophy that alarms so many in the gun rights community, as they see it as a symptom of a larger threat, the creation of a society in which personal liberty is usurped for "the common good."

As the late John Hosford would put it: "That's the day I'll *need* an AK-47."

CHAPTER 3

Extremist Groups and Media Complicity

Cleverly calling themselves "gun safety organizations," groups opposed to the private ownership of firearms and who want to see that fundamental civil right one day eviscerated have grown once again confident if not outright cocky, despite the June 2008 ruling by the United States Supreme Court in *District of Columbia v. Dick Anthony Heller* that the Second Amendment protects an individual citizen's right to own a gun.

These groups go by different names but their goals are common. For years, they strenuously argued that no such individual right existed or was protected by the Constitution, and they promoted and pushed for passage of statutes and ordinances based on that perspective. Now that this has failed, their next best hope is the appointment of federal judges and Supreme Court justices who will narrow that civil right dramatically, and the election of politicians to state and federal office who will legislate this important right to the level of irrelevance.

Who are these people?

The Brady Center to Prevent Gun Violence (aka The Brady Campaign to Prevent Gun Violence) was once known as Handgun Control, Inc. It is perhaps the largest of the anti-gun lobbies, and has under its umbrella the ill-fated, and numerically challenged, Million Mom March. In addition, the Brady Campaign is closely linked to various state-level "CeaseFire" organizations.

The change in name was to exploit the vicious attack on President Ronald Reagan and his entourage, which included Reagan press secretary James Brady, who was seriously wounded and left significantly disabled by gunman John Hinckley.

The Brady Campaign is affiliated with various state-level "CeaseFire" organizations, which promote gun control measures in legislatures and even at the local level. This group is well-funded and is arguably the most formidable opponent of gun rights organizations including the National Rifle Association, Second Amendment Foundation, Gun Owners of America and Citizens Committee for the Right to Keep and Bear Arms.

According to their website, the "Brady Center to Prevent Gun Violence and its legislative and grassroots affiliate, the Brady Campaign and its dedicated network of Million Mom March Chapters, is the nation's largest, non-partisan, grassroots organization leading the fight to prevent gun violence."

The group boasts that it is "devoted to creating an America free from gun violence, where all Americans are safe at home, at school, at work, and in our communities."

Next to the Brady group, the Violence Policy Center is perhaps the most vocal of the gun control lobbies. A tax-exempt 501(c)(3) non-profit organization based in Washington, DC, the VPC insists it works to reduce death by firearms through "research, advocacy and education."

Disingenuously telling America that "Guns and tobacco are the only two consumer products for which there is no federal health and safety oversight," the VPC neglects to mention that the firearms industry is one of the most heavily-regulated in the nation. Firearms and ammunition manufacturing are done under guidelines of the Sporting Arms and Ammunition Manufacturers' Institute, founded in 1926 at the request of the federal government. According to the SAAMI website, the organization has three chief tasks:

- Creating and publishing industry standards for safety, interchangeability, reliability and quality.
- Coordinating technical data.
- Promoting safe and responsible firearms use.

In addition to SAAMI oversight, firearms manufacturing and sales are monitored by the federal Bureau of Alcohol, Tobacco,

Firearms and Explosives (ATF), and gun purchasers must submit to a federal background check before they can take possession of a firearm purchased at retail.

There are thousands of federal, state and local gun laws. If one were to believe the organization's public claims, one would see the VPC as — according to its own website — "the most aggressive group in the gun control movement, (with) a record of policy successes on the federal, state, and local levels — including first revealing the threat posed by gun shows, drastically reducing the number of gun dealers, banning the possession of guns by domestic violence offenders, and exposing gun industry marketing to women and even children."

Another active group is the Coalition to Stop Gun Violence (GSGV). Similarly to the VPC, the Coalition "seeks to secure freedom from gun violence through research, strategic engagement and effective policy advocacy," according to its website.

"Our organizational structure is unique among national gun violence prevention organizations," the group states. "CSGV is comprised of 45 national organizations working to reduce gun violence. Our coalition members include religious organizations, child welfare advocates, public health professionals, and social justice organizations. This diversity of member organizations allows us to reach a wide variety of grassroots constituencies who share our vision of non-violence." Translation: These organizations are laboring strenuously to destroy the right to keep and bear arms and strip the Second Amendment from the framework of the Constitution.

One might observe at this point that the typical gun owner is also a firm believer in non-violence. The gun owner, however, has made the decision to not become a victim of violence, and has selected to react accordingly, in the event of life-threatening physical attack.

CSGV is led by perennial anti-rights gun prohibitionists Michael Beard and Joshua Horwitz.

The list of member organizations includes no surprises. Among this coalition are the American Academy of Pediatrics, American Jewish Committee and American Jewish Congress (they never heard of Warsaw?), Americans for Democratic Action, Children's Defense Fund, the DISARM Education Fund, Peace Action of Washington, National Urban League, Woman's National Democratic Club, United

States Student Association, United Methodist Church Board of Church & Society, and several other Leftist groups.

The San Francisco-based Legal Community Against Violence (LCAV) was created in the aftermath of the July 1, 1993 shooting that occurred in a San Francisco law firm that left ten people, including the gunman, dead and another six seriously wounded (one of them subsequently died).

LCAV was actively involved in pushing the 1994 Clinton ban on semiautomatic firearms. The group boasts that "Our services contributed to the adoption of hundreds of California firearms ordinances, many of which inspired state legislation that now places California at the forefront of gun policy reform."

In 1999, LCAV broadened its horizons by offering its services outside of California. Today, the group offers free assistance nationwide to gun control activists, and it has crafted model gun regulations for state and local governments around the country.

Perhaps not surprising to people who read our earlier book *America Fights Back: Armed Self-Defense in a Violent Age*, or who are familiar with Dr. John Lott's superb *The Bias Against Guns*, the thing that all of these anti-gun organizations and coalitions have in common beyond their revulsion to gun rights, firearms and the people who own them is that all get tacit if not outright support from major news organs.

In the April 2000 issue of *Reason*, writer Jacob Sullum observed, "Anyone who regularly watches television news will not be surprised by the general conclusion of a recent Media Research Center study: TV reporters do not like guns."

The center analyzed news coverage relating to firearms and found that the three major networks, ABC, NBC and CBS, along with CNN, looked at 653 "gun policy stories." What the center found, and Sullum dutifully noted, was that "those (stories) advocating more gun control outnumbered stories opposing gun control by 357 to 36, or a ratio of almost 10 to 1."

The remaining 260 stories were declared "neutral," meaning that they were fairly balanced.

Of course, there has long been an axiom in news that "if it bleeds, it leads." There is nothing like a hard-hitting, dramatic story about a murder, violent rape (is there really any other kind of rape?), armed robbery with shots fired, a drive-by shooting, a shooting involving cops and bad guys; anything that alarms the public.

Notably absent in this list of reasons to broadcast a story is a good self-defense situation where an armed private citizen successfully defends himself or herself against a violent crime. Rarely does such a story lead a news broadcast or find its way to the front page of a metropolitan daily newspaper.

Further confirmation of this phenomenon can be found even earlier than Lott's work. In an article headlined "Guns Save Lives," author Thomas Sowell wrote in *Issues & Views* in the Summer/Fall 1999 edition that "Every story about a child killed by a gun is front page news. Stories about lives saved by guns are lucky to appear in the second section of the newspaper and can just about forget it as far as appearing on CBS, ABC, NBC or CNN."

In a speech before a national leadership gathering for Hillsdale College, held in Seattle, Washington on May 25, 2004, Lott – then a resident scholar at the American Enterprise Institute – observed, "People are very surprised to learn that survey data show that guns are used defensively by private citizens in the U.S. from 1.5 to 3.4 million times a year, at least three times more frequently than guns are used to commit crimes. A question I hear repeatedly is: 'If defensive gun use occurs so often, why haven't I ever heard of even one story'?"

Why, indeed?

According to Lott, a survey he conducted in November 2002 of 1,015 people suggested that about 2.3 million defensive uses of firearms occurred during the previous year. He said larger surveys had produced essentially the same results. But where are the news reports of such incidents? Why does the mainstream press ignore these legitimate defensive gun uses?

Most of the time, a shot is not even fired, Lott explained.

"Though my survey indicates that simply brandishing a gun stops crimes 95 percent of the time," he told the audience, "it is very rare to see a story of such an event reported in the media. A dead gunshot victim on the ground is highly newsworthy, while a criminal fleeing after a woman points a gun is often not considered news at all."

If it *doesn't* bleed, it doesn't lead.

"Even though fewer than one out of 1,000 defensive gun uses result in the death of the attacker," Lott continued, "the newsman's penchant for drama means that the bloodier cases are usually covered. Even in the rare cases in which guns are used to shoot someone, injuries are about six times more frequent than deaths. You wouldn't know this from the stories the media choose to report."

Yet, the lack of drama does not entirely explain away the habitual ignorance of pro-gun stories that reflect the positive use of a privately-owned firearm. Lott suggested that the problem is with the reporters, themselves, and their bosses. These people may have personal and political biases against guns, they may be deliberately ignorant of firearms, and they find it shocking that their fellow citizens might resort to using guns to stop a violent crime.

In the aftermath of a shooting at the Appalachian Law School in Virginia in January 2002, Lott found only four stories out of a total of more than 200 in the week after the event that mentioned the shooter had been confronted by two armed students. In his remarks to the Hillsdale Leadership audience, Lott recalled, "The *Kansas City Star* printed a particularly telling interview with Jack Stokes, media relations manager at the Associated Press, who 'dismissed accusations that news groups deliberately downplayed the role gun owners may have played in stopping' the shooting. But Stokes 'did acknowledge being 'shocked' upon learning that students carrying guns had helped subdue the gunman. 'I thought, my God, they're putting into jeopardy even more people by bringing out these guns'."

Author Workman is a professional journalist who likes to explain to other reporters that "guns are my beat." This puts the firearms issue in terms most reporters can relate to, much the same as "city government is my beat" or "health care is my beat." This translates to "guns are my particular area of expertise." It accounts for why he occasionally is contacted by other journalists around the country not only for comment on a gun-related issue, but also to explain the differences between certain types of firearms, or what the issues are surrounding a particular class of firearms, such as the .50 BMG caliber rifles that are frequently demonized by gun control groups.

He is rare in the world of journalism, where the majority of reporters know little if anything about firearms. They do not own them, never wanted one and all-too-frequently have a somewhat apprehensive if not downright jaundiced opinion of average gun owners.

In fairness, some gun owners can be their own worst enemies, and are horrible examples for the shooting community. On internet forums, they spell poorly, they use poor grammar in letters to the editor, and in public they are not very careful about their personal appearance or demeanor, or even what they say and how they say it. Such examples, while they hardly represent the mainstream firearms community, leave a poor impression with journalists who go away believing more strongly that their preconceived notions about gun owners as knuckle-dragging Neanderthals are entirely accurate.

Living down to a cartoonist's stereotype of a beer-bellied, marginally literate hick who spends more money on guns than groceries for his family is hardly the way to convince the public that firearms owners are responsible and do not need to be subject to burdensome regulations.

Still, one could argue that bias against stereotypes seems to be rather exclusively reserved for gun owners.

As author Sowell, quoted earlier in this chapter, noted in his 1999 "Guns Save Lives" article, "If the media will report, we the citizens and voters can decide. But the media remain wedded to one side of this issue – the gun-control side – and wedded still moreso to presenting news as one interest group versus another, rather than informing the public about the facts, regardless of which side it helps or hurts."

Alas, if one subscribes to Lott's argument that there is a distinct bias against beneficial uses of firearms, particularly in self-defense cases, then the press is never going to give gun ownership a fair shake.

Fairness becomes even more elusive when gun rights advocates appear as guests on cable television news channels, typically in a debate scenario with someone from the gun control lobby. In many cases, the commentator or host of the program also takes sides, the majority of the time against the gun advocate.

Perhaps no better examples of this pattern surfaced in April 2009 for author Gottlieb, who is founder of the Second Amendment Foundation and chairman of the Citizens Committee for the Right to Keep and Bear Arms. Gottlieb had been invited to appear on MSNBC's *Hardball* program with substitute host David Schuster in the wake of several high-profile shooting incidents, to discuss why so many Americans had been buying firearms and ammunition at record rates.

However, Gottlieb had hardly begun to speak during his April 6 appearance when Schuster began interrupting and "talking over" him. That same rude conduct did not extend to Schuster's other guest, Charles Blow of the *New York Times*, who had authored a column decrying the availability of handguns to private citizens. The program segment became something of a shouting match between Schuster and Gottlieb, and resulted in a torrent of vile hate (male) to the gun rights advocate, which will be discussed in a later chapter.

The following day, Gottlieb was on television again, this time with CNN's Rich Sanchez. Once again, the commentator repeatedly interrupted Gottlieb.

There is a point where "probing journalism" becomes rude and abusive advocacy, and that line is crossed all-too-frequently by broadcast advocates disguising themselves as journalists.

Jeff Johnson, the congressional bureau chief for CNSNews.com wrote in October 2003 about "The Media's Intentional Bias Against Guns." He quoted Lott's research, noting that "In an examination of *New York Times* stories from 2001, Lott found 104 articles related to the use of guns by criminals, totaling 50,745 words…By contrast, the national 'newspaper of record' wrote 163 words about the defensive use of a gun by a citizen in only one story. The results were similar for *USA Today*, which reported 5,660 words on criminal use of guns but no reporting on the use of guns to stop crimes, and the *Washington Post*, which devoted 46,884 words to the criminal use of firearms and 953 words to their defensive use by law-abiding citizens."

Lott, himself, also cited another symptom of the media bias, and that is what the firearms community might consider the "unholy alliance" between the press and gun control groups mentioned earlier in this chapter.

"Another sign of bias," Lott noted in his Seattle speech, "is in the choice of authorities quoted. An analysis of *New York Times* news articles over a two-year period shows that *Times* reporters overwhelmingly cite pro-gun control academics in their articles. From February 2000 to February 2002, the *Times* cited nine strongly pro-control academics a total of 20 times; one neutral academic once; and no academic who was skeptical that gun control reduces crime.

"It's not that anti-control academics are non-existent," he continued. "In 1999, 294 academics from institutions as diverse as Harvard, Stanford, Northwestern, the University of Pennsylvania and UCLA released an open letter to Congress stating that the new gun laws being proposed at that time were 'ill-advised.' None of these academics was quoted in *New York Times* reports on guns over a two-year period."

It seems insufficient for the press to merely slant its news coverage against legitimate gun usage, and to overload its source pool with gun control advocates, reporters almost invariably include adjectives in their stories solely for the purpose of demonizing firearms. For example, it is rare when some report of a crime committed with a semiautomatic rifle does not identify the gun as "a high powered assault rifle." The term is both inflammatory and wrong.

Semiautomatic look-alikes of military firearms are not true "assault rifles." They are simply semiautomatic rifles that function identically to popular hunting and competition rifles that have been in use for almost a century. They merely "look" different, perhaps menacing to the untrained eye, because they have black synthetic stocks and long magazines. Still, these rifles can fire only one round with every squeeze of the trigger.

The press conveniently neglects to explain this, and frequently shows stock archive footage of fully-automatic machine guns being fired for visual effect when discussing the semi-auto firearms that are central to their stories. This journalistic sleight of hand is simply deceptive, and is done either deliberately, or out of total ignorance.

As we discussed in the previous chapter, these guns are hardly "high powered" in nature. The typical AR-15 fires a .223 Remington/5.56mm NATO cartridge that was designed primarily for shooting prairie dogs, woodchucks and coyotes. The AK-type rifles fire a 7.62x39mm cartridge, which is about as powerful ballistically as the .30-30 Winchester or .300 Savage cartridges, which are common hunting cartridges for deer. Far more powerful cartridges are also used by deer and elk hunters all over the map.

Instead of offering such a detail, or simply omitting references to "high-powered" guns, the press perpetuates the erroneous stereotype.

The same "high-powered" label would almost certainly be applied to a modified Ruger 10/22 rifle, possibly the most popular semiautomatic .22-caliber rimfire rifle in production anywhere in the world, if it were fitted with custom options that changed its appearance. This small-caliber rifle is so popular that a cottage industry has arisen over the years to produce any number of replacement parts and accessories, from heavy target-grade barrels to rugged folding or one-piece synthetic stocks or fancy wood stocks made from exotic woods or laminates.

Yet the cartridge for the 10/22 remains the same, the .22 Long Rifle, a tiny rimfire cartridge that is primarily used for small game, rodent control and Olympic-style competition shooting or other competitive matches. The appearance of the rifle, when equipped with a black synthetic folding stock tends to alarm people, yet the gun never changes mechanically from one incarnation to the next. It may be fitted with an extended magazine, but all that really does is enable the recreational shooter to go through his ammunition far quicker.

There is an alarming willingness on the part of reporters to accept without challenge how gun control groups classify virtually any firearm they want to vilify on any given day. Today, it might be the .50-caliber rifle discussed in the previous chapter. Tomorrow, one of these groups may decide to go after someone's hunting rifle because it is fitted with a telescopic sight and a synthetic stock rather than a fancy checkered wood stock.

Many of today's popular hunting rifles are built at the factory with synthetic stocks and subsequently fitted with scopes. The gun control lobby might decide to label such guns as "sniper rifles" with no basis other than the material used and the type of sight. Such guns are now in use all over the world by sport hunters, who have harmed nobody. Their use in crime is so infrequent as to not even register on the charts.

Woe unto a sportsman who also adds a bipod for a more stable shot, for his gun would now fall well within the definition – based solely on cosmetics – of an evil "sniper rifle."

A reporter looking for a sensational story seems always willing to do one on some newly-attacked firearm.

An example of this surfaced in October 2008 when ABC's Neal Karlinsky, reporting from Wyoming for Good Morning America, used statistics from the Violence Policy Center to illustrate his piece, as though this was the definitive data on the subject. There was no data from the NRA or any other pro-gun rights group included in the report, which was published by News Busters.

The problem faced by gun control lobbyists is they cannot seem to always get their stories straight.

Paul Helmke, president of the Brady Campaign to Prevent Gun Violence, remarked during an October 28, 2008 debate on gun laws for National Public Radio that "32 people are killed with guns, murdered with guns every day in this country."

"There's a Virginia Tech happening every day in this country," he said matter-of-factly.

However, according to the Coalition to Stop Gun Violence. using data from the National Education Association's Health Information Network, more than 80 Americans die from gun violence."

In the same discussion, Helmke told the audience, "Statistics show that if you've got a gun in your home, it is 22 times more likely to be used against you or a family member."

Yet, according to the Violence Policy Center's website, "Having a gun in the home makes it three times more likely that you or someone you care about will be murdered by a family member or intimate partner."

Well, which is it? Are we killing 32 or 80 people a day with firearms? Are we three times or 22 times more likely to die from a gunshot wound if we keep a firearm in the home?

Yet another twist to this dilemma comes in the way firearms fatalities are classified by age group, with gun control proponents — including the Centers for Disease and Control (CDC) — habitually combining children and adolescents, and young adults, into the "children" category, presumably to boost the statistics for gun-related fatalities.

For example, the CDC reported, "Firearm deaths for children and teens dropped significantly between 1997 and 1998 according to a new mortality report released today by the U.S. Department of Health and Human Services. The report shows 3,792 children and adolescents under age 20 died in 1998 from firearms, down 10 percent from 4,223 in 1997, and down 35 percent from the high of 5,833 in 1994."

But then the website Scott Counseling noted, "In the U.S. for 2001, there were 29,573 deaths from firearms, distributed as follows by mode of death: Suicide 16,869; Homicide 11,348. During that same time period, 802 individuals died due to accidental gun related deaths. Half the victims involved were children (individuals under 18 years of age)."

Defining children and separating them from adolescents and teenagers seems an impossible task to those inclined to encourage anti-gun hysteria.

Leave it to Dr. Lott to bring the debate back into perspective, as he did with his remarks to the Hillsdale College audience in Seattle.

"(T)he annual number of accidental gun deaths involving children under ten - most of these being cases where someone older shoots the child - is consistently a single digit number," Lott observed, while clearly defining who "children" really are. "It is a kind of media archetype story to report on 'naturally curious' children shooting themselves or other children - though in the five years from 1997 to 2001 the entire United States averaged only ten cases a year where a child under ten accidentally shot himself or another child.

"In contrast," Lott added for further perspective, "in 2001 bicycles were much more likely to result in accidental deaths than guns. Fully 93 children under the age of ten drowned accidentally in bathtubs. Thirty-six children under five drowned in buckets in 1998. Yet few reporters crusade against buckets or bathtubs."

Clearly, people and groups with specific agendas can take data and combine it, redefine it and come up with a conclusion that supports any argument they wish to make. Lott, however, is an economist and what he does is crunch numbers. While he has been cast in the role of a pro-gun advocate, he only has the data with which to work.

For many years, the press has not simply warmed up to, but accepted without question or even cursory analysis, such compiled and compressed data from gun control organizations as veritable gospel. When the press takes sides on an issue — and usually it is the liberal/Left side of an issue, whether it is gun control, a presidential election or taxes — they are loathe to ever acknowledge having made a mistake, much less admit they have taken sides and presented a biased story.

This is perhaps where the Internet has played its most important role. Because the public now has virtually instant access to data from many different sources, Americans no longer have to simply rely upon what they read in the newspaper or hear on a television. They can consult data quoted by various sources, and make up their own minds which statistics are accurate.

This access also allows people to get past the volatile rhetoric in which the Brady Campaign's Helmke and his contemporaries engage, including this remark delivered during the NPR debate: "People don't realize just how weak our gun laws are in this country. We basically allow almost anyone to get any kind of a gun."

This and similar statements are common fodder from gun prohibitionists and they reinforce the myth that American gun laws need to be far more restrictive. Such restrictions, of course, are designed to reduce a fundamental civil right to the level of a highly-regulated privilege.

Besides, the assertion is fundamentally false. We do not "basically allow almost anyone to get any kind of a gun." There are prohibitions on lawful gun ownership, and Helmke knows this. Convicted felons, persons under indictment, persons with histories of illegal drug use, persons with histories of mental problems who have been adjudicated mentally unstable, persons under court protection orders; none of these people may legally purchase or possess a firearm.

However, any law-abiding citizen with a clean record can, indeed, purchase and possess a firearm, as many as they want, provided they obey local statutes in the process. For example, if their state has a one-handgun-per-month law, then they can only purchase a single handgun during any 30-day period.

Helmke also said this: "Rather than voting to say that guns reduce crime, you should stop and think that restricting access to guns is what would reduce crime."

Invariably, these people always insist they are not against gun ownership. They simply want to regulate that ownership so tightly as to discourage people from every owning a firearm.

There is yet another manifestation of media bias against firearms, and that is in the realm of commercial advertising. Many newspapers around the country have adopted advertising policies that reject advertisements for handguns. This applies to display advertising as well as classified advertising. The same policy may, depending upon the particular newspaper, apply to so-called "assault weapons," but the primary target of this anti-gun advertising prohibition is the handgun.

Newspapers will typically accept advertising for traditional "sporting rifles" and shotguns, and for ammunition sales, but even in the wake of a Supreme Court ruling that declared handguns to be legitimate weapons protected under the Second Amendment, those bastions of First Amendment protectionism balk and turn up their corporate noses. From a strictly business perspective, this prohibitionist approach makes no sense at all, because in the final analysis, newspapers are turning their backs on advertising income. Call it some sort of adherence to some lofty self-established "higher moral ground," but one would strain the limits of credulity to argue that rejecting handgun advertising is acceptable while it would be considered wholly inappropriate to disallow advertising from adult bookstores, porn shops or abortion clinics.

The contention that sales of handguns through classified advertisements would allow criminals to avoid background checks does not stand up under even the most cursory scrutiny, because those same newspapers will generally allow classified advertising for long guns. A criminal with a hour to spare, and a sharp hacksaw, can shorten the barrel of any shotgun he may purchase through a private transaction for illegal purposes.

Some newspapers may also reject advertising for gun shows, and in that regard, newspapers are not alone in their disdain of anything firearm-related. One example of this would be in Seattle, Washington where, after years of running monthly advertisements for gun shows conducted by the Washington Arms Collectors, Fisher Broadcasting, the parent company of KVI, a conservative AM talk radio station, cancelled a long running contract with the gun collectors group. The arms collectors took their money to a rival conservative talk radio station, and also ran advertisements on at least one country music FM station.

If one is looking for hypocrisy in the press, look no farther than a newspaper with an editorial stance calling for background checks at all gun shows. If those newspapers accept any kind of classified advertising for firearms, they are engaging in essentially the same practice of promoting gun sales without background checks. In the interest of consistency, a newspaper cannot logically accept classified advertising for the private sale of any firearms, while rejecting advertising for gun shows; especially gun shows where sales are limited to members of an organization who must first be screened before they are granted membership status.

The press, and especially newspaper management and editorial boards, have perhaps convinced themselves that their philosophical adherence to the agendas of such groups as the Brady Campaign and Violence Policy Center is for the "common good." This is dangerous ground to tread, however, because it evidently escapes those people that the First Amendment, upon which they rest not only their principles but their living, is in as much jeopardy of erosion as is the Second Amendment, which they are so eagerly devoted to helping erode.

It may someday occur to an editor or reporter that all civil rights are equal, and that one cannot acquiesce to the piecemeal destruction of one without opening the floodgate to the eventual surrender of them all.

CHAPTER 4

Punishing the Innocent

During the 37-year history of Seattle, Washington's Folklife Festival held at the Seattle Center – the site of that city's 1962 World's Fair – there had never been a dangerously violent incident. Certainly, there had been arrests for public intoxication and other minor offenses, but until the spring of 2008, not a shot had been fired and nobody had been seriously hurt as the result of a criminal act.

The festival is something of an annual homage to the hippie generation of a bygone era and a somewhat self-imposed tribute by, and to, Seattle's Establishment Left. It is normally a rather harmless gathering of people who never quite grew out of the protest movement of the 1960s. That said, the festival has a history of being rather laid back, and almost everyone mellows out and gets along with one another.

That record changed with a fight that erupted between one armed man named Clinton Chad Grainger of Snohomish County and another man. Grainger, licensed to carry a concealed handgun despite what was later described as a history of mental problems – though that history apparently did not appear during a background check on Grainger by the Snohomish County Sheriff's Department, which issued the carry license – was carrying a Glock pistol in an ankle holster.

The other man apparently spotted the gun, there was some pushing and then things got quickly got out of hand. Grainger and the other man began wrestling over his pistol. During the altercation, the gun discharged, slightly injuring the man Grainger was fighting, and more seriously wounding another man identified as Joshua Penaluna in the wrist and his girlfriend, Sarah Thorsnes, in the leg.

Put this in perspective: Months after the non-fatal shooting, South Seattle neighborhoods erupted in a surge of gang violence. It reached a fever pitch in November 2008 after a highly-publicized fatal gang-related shooting at the Southcenter Mall in Tukwila, a Seattle suburb.

Yet in the summer of 2008, Seattle's liberal Democrat Mayor Greg Nickels, a founding member of "Mayors Against Illegal Guns" with New York Mayor Michael Bloomberg and Boston Mayor Thomas Menino, launched a campaign that polarized not just his community but the entire state. Nickels announced that he would issue an executive order banning handguns, even those carried by legally-licensed citizens, from all city property, including parks, libraries and other public buildings and, of course, the Seattle Center. This was not because of the gang violence plaguing Seattle's minority neighborhoods, but because of an incident at the Folklife Festival that happened in the heartland of Seattle's Establishment liberals, and in the shadow of the city's upscale Queen Anne neighborhood.

Mayor Nickels did not call upon his police department, under the leadership of then-Chief Gil Kerlikowske – whose personal Glock 9mm was stolen out of his parked, unmarked city car the day after Christmas 2005 – to clean the gangs out of Seattle's Central District, West Seattle or Rainier Valley. He went after guns carried by law-abiding citizens who had gone through background checks to obtain a state concealed pistol license (CPL), the overwhelming majority of whom had harmed nobody, and statistically have a lower incidence of any kind of criminal violation including speeding tickets than the population at large.

Nickels pushed this ban despite being strongly advised in writing by the State Attorney General's office that under Washington statute, he did not have the authority to impose such a restriction.

Washington has one of the nation's oldest, and most copied, state preemption laws. That is, the State Legislature retains sole authority on firearms regulation within the state's borders. It has been a remarkably efficient law, which has the same effect in Spokane as it does in Seattle. State residents and visitors are not faced with a checkerboard scenario where gun laws change from one community to another, and where a person may have a gun legally in one jurisdiction but he becomes a criminal by simply crossing a boundary into a neighboring jurisdiction.

Under this law, and the state's concealed carry statutes, prohibitions proposed by Nickels or anyone else in municipal government must carry with them an exemption for licensed citizens, and those local ordinances may not be more restrictive than the state law.

Nickels, a strong ally of the Northwest's most hysteria-driven gun control group, Washington CeaseFire, angered people outside of the firearms community when he said this ban would be accomplished by "executive order" instead of passing it before the city council as a proposed ordinance. In short, there would be no legislative review, the mayor would simply decree that all guns are banned on city property and "that would be that."

This would be a deliberate test of the Legislature's mettle, and the statute that had been in effect for a generation. If Nickels could defy state law and get away with it, then anti-gun mayors in other Washington communities could follow suit. The underlying intent, of course, was to fracture the state preemption statute, a trophy prize for the gun control movement, because if they could destroy one of the country's oldest and well-established such laws, they would be able to challenge similar laws in other states.

Why this effort to challenge state authority on gun laws? The strategy is to undermine common-sense gun laws, and firearm civil rights, so that ultimately, through passage of local ordinances, gun ownership would become so cumbersome that citizens would become discouraged and decide that owning firearms – even though it is a constitutionally-protected civil right – simply isn't worth the hassle.

Targeting law-abiding gun owners when gangs and criminal activity are seemingly rampant is a cowardly cop-out, according to critics of such laws in the gun rights community. Metropolitan leaders like Greg Nickels and former Police Chief Gil Kerlikowske – an ardent supporter of tougher gun laws and an opponent of shall-issue/right-to-carry laws that require CPLs be issued to any citizen who passes a background check and meets the standards – want to control who has guns. They also want it to appear as though they are actually taking action against crime, and what better way to convince people of their efforts than to disarm the public?

Except in this case, the wrong people would be disarmed. Teenage thugs and gang-bangers cannot legally carry concealed handguns anywhere, whether in Seattle, Philadelphia, Boston, New York City, Detroit, Milwaukee or Los Angeles. But instead of going after these dangerous gangsters, Nickels and others like him launch their attacks against legally-armed citizens who would never consider deliberately harming someone else in a premeditated criminal attack.

While Seattle might have been something of a test, it was not the only municipality that launched this sort of gun ban campaign in 2008. Indeed, the strategy turned up in enough places around the country that a conspiracy theorist might be giddy with paranoia.

The City of Clyde, Ohio had tried to ban guns in public parks and other places, and it took a ruling by the Ohio Supreme Court to strike down the ban.

Two communities in West Virginia, Martinsburg and Ranson, also considered such bans, causing Mountain State gun rights activists to react loudly. Officials in South Bend, Indiana also looked at such a ban. The common denominator with all of these proposals was an official viewpoint that average citizens could not be trusted with defensive firearms in public places where they had a right to be.

In the small city of Montesano, Washington located about 100 miles southwest from Seattle, the council adopted an ordinance banning legally-carried guns on public property, but the mayor promptly vetoed the measure. Unlike his big city counterpart, the Montesano mayor recognized publicly that such an ordinance would violate the state preemption statute.

Adopting gun control ordinances and statutes that affect only law-abiding citizens is nothing new. Claims by proponents that such laws keep guns out of the hands of criminals have been proven false time and again by crime statistics and by anecdotal evidence involving individual recidivist offenders. Almost invariably, such persons are able to secure firearms for their criminal activities, and to defend themselves against other criminals.

An interesting study into this problem was published by the Department of Justice under the title *Violent Encounters: A Study of Felonious Assaults on Our Nation's Law Enforcement Officers*. The study was done by Anthony J. Pinizzotto, Ph.D., Edward F. Davis, M.S., both with the FBI's Training and Development Division, Behavioral Science Unit, and Charles E. Miller, III with the FBI's Criminal Justice Information Services Division, Training and Systems Education Unit. It was released in August 2006 to rather scant review, perhaps because it contained the following information:

The study looked at several violent offenders and discovered that "None of the rifles, shotguns, or handguns connected with this study were obtained from gun shows or related activities." (Page 51)

On the following page was this revelation: "When asked about the ease of obtaining firearms illegally, one offender in the current study said:

"All these politicians are screaming about more gun laws, more gun laws. F— the gun laws. I never gave a sh— about the gun laws that are on the books. And the 8,000 new gun laws would have made absolutely, whatsoever, about me getting a gun. Why? Because I never went into a gun store or to a gun show or to a pawn shop or anyplace else where firearms are legally bought and sold and picked up a gun, ever. Because I'm a felon, I couldn't pass a background check, you know…" (Page 52)

One might reasonably conclude that in today's environment with certain crimes and gang activity on the increase, thanks in no small part to budget cuts in local law enforcement, that now is not the time to disarm private citizens or discourage them from protecting themselves and their families. Encouraging gun ownership and the use of firearms in self-defense is hardly part of the philosophy at the root of gun control measures.

President Barack Obama earned no credit for himself among right-to-carry advocates when, on the campaign trail in Pittsburg, Pennsylvania early in 2008, he told a reporter for the *Pittsburgh Tribune-Review*, "I am not in favor of concealed weapons. I think that creates a potential atmosphere where more innocent people could (get shot during) altercations."

The remark ignited a small firestorm among gun rights activists, and the Citizens Committee for the Right to Keep and Bear Arms demanded a public apology from Obama, which of course never came.

But Mr. Obama's rhetoric against concealed carry could hardly compare to the condescension exhibited by California Congressman Henry Waxman, a perennial anti-gun Liberal Democrat who once observed, "If someone is so fearful that, that they're going to start using their weapons to protect their rights, (it) makes me very nervous that these people have these weapons at all."

There is a colorable argument that Rep. Waxman has forgotten that the Second Amendment to the U.S. Constitution was included in the Bill of Rights for just such a reason. Gun rights advocates, and many historians, concur that the "right of the people to keep and bear arms" was specified in the Bill of Rights purposely as something of an "insurance policy" against government tyranny. So long as the people have arms, they can resist tyranny and "protect their rights," as Mr. Waxman seems to have lamented.

Waxman is an example of far too many individuals, typically but not always Liberals, who ascend to public office and make a career out of it. So comfortable do they become in their positions of authority that the mere thought of the constituency throwing them out is something unsettling if not downright horrifying. Yet year after year, term after term, the Henry Waxman types on Capitol Hill – and there are a lot of them – and in state legislatures continually promote and pass legislation that tends to ratchet down on the very rights those armed citizens may wish to protect. Perhaps if they would not adopt onerous laws, people would not be so angry.

Angry or otherwise, the gun-owning public does not care to face more regulations on their gun ownership because a segment of the population – over whom they have no control – has chosen criminal pursuits in lieu of a more honest and productive occupation. Yet that is the nature of gun laws, or quasi-imperial decrees such as the one proposed by Seattle's Mayor Nickels; they effect the wrong people. Ironically, and with no small dose of hypocrisy, there is support for tightening down on the rights of gun owners from journalists who are quick to demand no such limitations on the First Amendment.

A sterling example of this double standard logic came from Charles Winokoor, a staff writer with GateHouse News Service on

November 20, 2008. In an article headline "Gun rights could stand more limitations," Winokoor held forth in the wake of a tragic gun mishap in Massachusetts in which an 8-year-old youngster died while trying to fire an Uzi submachine gun at a gun club during a special event.

Ignoring the rational approach of holding the boy's father, described as "a hospital emergency-department medical director," responsible for allowing his son to fire the gun without immediate physical assistance from a range master, Winokoor took the tack that so many other journalists have taken: Place limits on everyone because of the stupidity of a single individual who will pay for his lapse of judgment emotionally for the rest of his life.

But Winokoor first looks down his professional nose at the activity, a shoot at which participants could fire machine guns at pumpkins and other targets, observing, "How any sane adult, be they gun enthusiast or recreational hunter, could be a party to such a bizarre event is itself inexplicable." That may be true about anyone who has never participated in a fun shooting event, but to gun enthusiasts, such an event is considered great recreation.

Then Winokoor writes, "If I could submit a bill this January it would be one restricting anyone from buying an assault weapon unless first undergoing a special training course, something that in a perfect world the NRA would stand behind."

He also reported that at least one state representative was planning to draft a bill essentially doing just that very thing, and making it illegal for anyone under age 21 from legally firing an automatic weapon. Presumably he had not taken this up with the commander of the Massachusetts National Guard or the Marines, Army or Navy units stationed in the state.

But from a single tragedy, like the single shooting at Seattle's Folklife Festival, Winokoor would impose a statute that essentially punishes every citizen for the malfeasance of one parent, and misbehavior of one questionable individual at a public gathering.

Nothing could be more telling about the holier-than-thou approach to gun rights than this passage in Winokoor's column: "I know, I know. It's our Second Amendment right to bear arms and protect ourselves and our property ("The British are coming, the British are coming!"), and God bless the National Rifle Association for going that extra mile to ensure our freedom to amass a personal arsenal and fire at will.

"With apologies to the late Charlton Heston, I just don't get it."

Gun rights advocates would be in total agreement with Winokoor on that last admission. He doesn't "get it."

Gun control advocates see the world as operating on their terms, and any variation is unacceptable. Behavior that they view with apprehension is to be strictly regulated or prohibited entirely, and that especially goes for firearms ownership and use. Despite claims to the contrary, strict proponents of gun control – and this goes especially for those who admit to owning their own firearms – are simply not comfortable with the notion of widespread gun ownership "among the masses." Yes, they have *their* firearms, but they typically keep them locked up and put away, fearful they may have an accident, or more fearful that one of their friends might discover they own a gun.

Here, again, is a notorious double standard. A class of gun owners having appointed themselves as referees of gun ownership standards finds no objection to regulations on other gun owners, provided of course that the adopted regulations correspond to their own self-established doctrines.

That may or may not be worse than the notion of non-gun owners setting standards they believe to be entirely reasonable, but if put into actual practice would – and in some cases have – rendered firearms ownership to the level of a restricted privilege. It would be tantamount to allowing someone to purchase an automobile that he or she could never drive, except under very strict guidelines, the violation of which could cost that person his or her driving privileges for life.

Of course people make mistakes with firearms. Some behave so egregiously that even gun owners have been merciless in their condemnations.

Ample proof of this was the aftermath of a case in Washington State in November 2008 in which a man began cleaning his firearms after first having downed several shots of vodka. He sent his 6-year-old daughter to his bedroom to retrieve a loaded .45-caliber semiautomatic pistol. After removing the magazine, he squeezed the trigger, apparently without confirming that the gun's chamber was empty. The child was struck point blank in the head by a single projectile and died.

Even the staunchest gun rights advocates agree that such individuals deserve to suffer whatever the law allows, for to handle firearms when one is clearly intoxicated is a violation of every gun safety rule known to man.

However, these individuals should suffer the consequences all by themselves, the firearms community maintains. Gun advocates argue that it is irrational to push for statutes that tend to micro-manage firearms handling, and impose those requirements on everyone. Such efforts are guaranteed to have two failures: They do not affect the behavior of people who will ignore the law, and they do not bring back from the dead the victim whose misfortune led to pressure for adoption of the new law.

On the rare occasions when gun rights advocates and gun prohibitionists agree, it is over programs that result in the incarceration of armed violent criminals. Such was the case when the National Rifle Association and Brady Campaign to Prevent Gun Violence actually supported a law in Virginia that put armed criminals in prison, brought down the murder rate in Richmond after ten years, and essentially did not interfere with the lawful carrying of handguns, either concealed or openly, by law-abiding residents.

Virginia is an "open carry" state and there is an active open carry movement. Though they are still very much in the minority among gun owners, the "OCers," as they call themselves, have initiated something of a revival of a practice that went out of vogue more than a century ago except in some areas of the west. Much to the surprise of authorities in many states, open carry is not illegal, these OC advocates have discovered. While the practice is anachronistic, it is allowed by law and in some cases protected by state constitutions.

The "down side" of this practice is that it tends to leave many people even more uneasy about armed citizens. The fact that none of these OCers has engaged in a criminal act is overlooked by those who are simply stunned to see anyone in the 21st Century strolling around with a gun on his or her hip.

This practice is not necessarily given blanket approval in the firearms community. At the 2008 Gun Rights Policy Conference, an annual project of the Second Amendment Foundation and Citizens Committee for the Right to Keep and Bear Arms, attorney Scott Hattrup of Kansas was critical of open carry.

"Open carry, in my view, is primarily a political statement," he stated. "Even in western states where it's still a common occurrence, open carry is primarily a political statement."

This may not go down well with OCers, who contend that they are merely exercising a civil right and something of an abandoned practice. That the appearance of visibly armed private citizens alarms some people seems of no consequence to the OC movement, which simply reacts to criticism with a "get over it" philosophy.

To his credit, Hattrup observed that OCers "want to desensitize folks that are out there that see the guns being carried on the hips of everyday citizens and get them used to the concept that gun owners are a majority of Americans."

Ironically, Hattrup's home state was one of the first to have gun control laws west of the Mississippi, dating all the way back to the days of Wyatt Earp and the big cattle drive era. Remarkably, according to historical accounts from writers such as Richard Shenkman, author of *Legends, Lies and Cherished Myths of American History*, and Ryan McMaken, author of *The American West: A Heritage of Peace*, there really were not a lot of homicides in that era. Contrary to the myth created by Hollywood and now perpetuated by gun control advocates in their opposition to concealed carry statutes, the Old West was not marked by a great deal of promiscuous or widespread gunplay.

Yes, there were range wars that were violent and costly in terms of human life. The Johnson County War in Wyoming, the Lincoln County War in New Mexico that made a legend of "Billy the Kid" Bonney, and the battle between the Earp clan and the Clanton-McLaury cowboys that led to the fabled Gunfight at the O.K. Corral, the outlaw activities of the James-Younger gang and the Daltons resulted in considerable body counts. But they were the aberration, not the norm, and one might argue that open carry of firearms had as much to do with keeping everyone's behavior somewhat in check, as did tough lawmen whose activities and reaction to crime were not hamstrung by complex laws and lawsuit-happy attorneys.

Is it that today's open carry activists wish to return to those days of old, when people could leave their doors unlocked, or are they simply out for a reaction?

"You have to think about what your goals are when you are carrying openly," Hattrup said during his remarks in Phoenix, Arizona.

"Is your ultimate goal to protect that practice or is your ultimate goal just to scare some people and keep them off your back?"

All of this said, there is no indication that OCers pose any threat to the public, other than to visually assault the sensitivities of citizens unused to the visible carry of firearms.

However, in far too many cases where law enforcement is not "well schooled" in the law, there have been unpleasant confrontations between these law-abiding citizens and some police officers. The trouble has sometimes escalated in wrongful detention and arrest, leading to embarrassing apologies at the very least, and occasionally to civil rights lawsuits. One man in Louisiana was turned into an OC activist by his 2006 arrest and by the arrogant manner in which he apparently was treated by a local police chief. That resulted in an out-of-court settlement for an undisclosed sum.

In Pennsylvania, at least two civil rights lawsuits grew out of a single confrontation by OCers at a family restaurant in 2008.

Perhaps only in the state of Washington has an OC advocate been proactive by first contacting several local police and sheriff's agencies to remind them about open carry, resulting in a series of training bulletins issued by those departments to their officers. Still, there have been a few relatively minor confrontations between some OCers and police, but those situations have all ultimately been "sorted out" before the issue wound up in court.

Yet what has occurred here is a scenario in which law-abiding gun owners have been targeted when police resources might better be applied elsewhere, combating genuine crime.

In the process, many businesses have simply posted their private property off limits to any carrying of arms legally by their customers. Much of this has been the handiwork of insurance companies and corporate attorneys over liability concerns, real, imagined or conveniently invented simply as a form of discrimination against legal gun owners.

Whether it is discrimination in simply barring legally armed customers from a business, or it is of a more insidious nature – the passage of legislation – it still amounts to making the wrong people suffer for crimes or acts of negligence they did not commit.

There are unintended consequences for this sort of thing, as witnessed in the aftermath of tough gun law passage in other nations.

In 2008, WorldNetDaily reported that passage of restrictive gun ownership laws had resulted in a wave of killings in South Africa. People were stabbed, beaten, shot, raped and even burned alive.

In Great Britain, where gun ownership was severely restricted and handguns were banned following a school massacre in Dunblane, Scotland in 1996, violent crime has risen sharply. Shootings, stabbings and beatings had seemingly skyrocketed, and one victim was significant: Pat Regan, a leading gun control advocate. She was found stabbed to death in her home June 1. Five years ago, her son was fatally shot despite the handgun ban.

The *Evening Standard* reported at the time that "knife violence in London is now running as high as gun warfare in some U.S. cities." Stabbings had risen by 30 percent during the first six months of 2008, and it appeared crime was reaching epidemic proportions. At one point, the *Sunday Telegraph* reported that nearly 60 people were being attacked and mugged or stabbed every day in the United Kingdom, where acting in self-defense can get one thrown in prison.

Ask Tony Martin, the farmer who was sent to jail after he shot two burglars who had repeatedly broken into his home.

It is appalling to gun rights advocates that many Americans on the political Left think that the British model of gun regulation is the one that ought to apply in this country. Democrats, as a party, continue to cling to a philosophy that "reasonable" gun restrictions should be acceptable to gun owners.

A Harris Poll conducted in May 2008 revealed that a majority of people who identify themselves as Democrats want stricter gun control laws, even though there are thousands of laws already on the books and it is debatable that any of them have prevented a single crime. The Harris survey broke down the results to show that 70 percent of responding Democrats want more restrictions on handgun ownership, and 68 percent of them want greater restrictions on all firearms.

One significant measure these gun control proponents want to adopt is a law that would essentially regulate gun shows out of business, despite data compiled for the Department of Justice more than ten years ago that demonstrates gun shows are not the source of guns used by criminals. A survey of thousands of convicted felons found that less than one percent (0.7%) of them got their guns from gun shows.

More recently, a joint study by the University of Michigan and University of Maryland that examined suicide and homicide rates in California and Texas suggested strongly that gun shows do not contribute to deaths associated with either cause. That study, *The Effect of Gun Shows on Gun-Related Deaths: Evidence from California and Texas* by Mark Duggan and Randi Hjalmarsson from the University of Maryland and Brian A. Jacob at the University of Michigan, was released in mid-2008 and was immediately criticized and dismissed by gun control advocates.

The study authors noted, "We find no evidence that gun shows lead to substantial increases in either gun homicides or suicides. In addition, tighter regulation of gun shows does not appear to reduce the number of firearms-related deaths."

At some point it would be reasonable to expect American citizens to ask why, with ample research that suggests otherwise, gun control advocates in Congress and state legislatures would adhere to the notion that strictly regulating firearms, cracking down on gun shows and placing enormous burdens on gun owners is going to reduce violent crime.

The answer might be that it is far easier to regulate people who habitually obey the law than it is to take measures against people who habitually violate the law. Proponents of strict gun laws can adopt some pet measure, declare success and then move on to adopt a stronger regulation in the future when they discover – but would never admit – the one they just passed really has not stopped criminal activity.

CHAPTER 5

Legal, Political and Social Hypocrisy

Following the long-awaited ruling by the United States Supreme Court in the case of *District of Columbia v. Dick Anthony Heller* that the Second Amendment protected and affirmed an individual civil right to keep and bear arms, the American Civil Liberties Union reinforced its negative image among conservatives – and especially gun rights activists – as an organization that believes there are only nine amendments in the Bill of Rights.

Taking a position that infuriated many gun owners and merely confirmed the suspicions of others that the ACLU was only interested in *liberal* civil rights causes, the organization noted on its website, "The ACLU disagrees with the Supreme Court's conclusion about the nature of the right protected by the Second Amendment. We do not, however, take a position on gun control itself. In our view, neither the possession of guns nor the regulation of guns raises a civil liberties issue."

It doesn't? Owning firearms is a constitutionally-protected civil right, not only under the Second Amendment, but under the constitutions in a majority of states. One might legitimately ask the ACLU by what stretch of logic does the regulation of a civil right *not* become a civil liberties issue?

The ACLU's position reflects a disconnect between the traditional Left / Liberal philosophy about firearms and the majority of American citizens who have always believed that the Second

Amendment protected an individual right to own a gun. Its position on the *Heller* ruling only buttressed the belief that the ACLU has become just one more liberal anti-gun front group.

Rather than place itself in a position where it may one day have to defend the individual right of a citizen to have a gun in his or her home, or carry one on the street as a defense against criminal assault, the ACLU casually dismisses this right – which is also delineated in dozens of state constitutions – as lacking in civil liberties status. Were any other civil right at stake, such as free speech, freedom of the press, freedom of assembly, the right to remain silent or protection against illegal search and seizure, you can rest assured the ACLU would properly descend on the cause and the case like locusts. But because the Second Amendment protects the right to have a gun, the ACLU might loathe appearing in the same courtroom, unless perhaps it was representing the other side.

It might not have been so egregious a reaction from the ACLU, save for the fact that the organization issued a press statement that tried to re-write history, and was simply not true. While noting accurately that "The Second Amendment has not been the subject of much Supreme Court discussion through the years," the ACLU statement added, "To the extent it has been discussed, the Court has described the Second Amendment as designed to protect the ability of the states to preserve their own sovereignty against a new and potentially overreaching national government.

"Based on that understanding," the ACLU continued, "the Court has historically construed the Second Amendment as a collective right connected to the concept of a 'well-regulated militia' rather than an individual right to possess guns for private purposes."

For whatever reasons, the ACLU understands it wrong. In their concise book *Supreme Court Gun Cases*, attorneys David Kopel and Stephen Halbrook, and nationally-recognized firearms law expert Alan Korwin piece together a remarkably understandable history of gun rights that spans 200 years of American history, putting the lie to any argument that the courts have "always" held the view that the Second Amendment protected some imaginary right of states to organize militias.

The ACLU further contended, "In Heller, the Court reinterpreted the Second Amendment as a source of individual rights.

Washington D.C.'s gun control law, which bans the private possession of handguns and was widely considered the most restrictive such law in the country, became a victim of that reinterpretation."

The high court did no such thing. Rather, if one reads through *Supreme Court Gun Cases* and studies scholarly works from authorities ranging from Prof. Laurence Tribe to historian Clayton Cramer, it soon becomes obvious that the Supreme Court finally put the correct perspective on Second Amendment interpretation.

Justice Antonin Scalia's detailed analysis of the amendment and its history refute 70 years of misinterpretation. No matter how the ACLU or various anti-gun media pundits attempt to spin it, Scalia's majority opinion reveals the militia argument for what it is: utter nonsense.

Among conservatives, the gun rights issue has always been indicative of the greater philosophical chasm that exists on many social issues between themselves and liberals.

This rift manifests itself in many forms, not the least of which is a frequent observation about the irony of liberals being often hell bent against right-to-carry laws and so-called "castle doctrine" statutes, while strongly supporting abortion. The argument that liberals "are okay with killing unborn children but opposed to killing criminals in self-defense" has arisen in more than a few debates.

In recent years, gun rights advocates have taken many of the catch-phrases and buzz words often used by the liberal Left and turned them around to reinforce their own arguments. "Pro-choice" became the position supporting a woman's right to choose whether she would be raped and murdered, or be able to purchase a gun to protect herself from vicious criminal attack. A "sensible" gun law was one that mandated issuance of a concealed carry permit or license to any citizen who passed a criminal background check, thus removing the discretionary power of a judge or police chief. Such authority to dole out carry permits has all too frequently been abused by those in positions of power, and "shall issue" laws – passed invariably against the howling protests of the judges and police chiefs whose power was being stripped – became very popular among gun owners.

The gun control issue has been one steeped in hypocrisy for decades. Interestingly, in the days and weeks following the November 2008 election of Democrat Barack Obama as president of the United

States, countless numbers of people who had voted for him – evidently ignoring, or oblivious to, his anti-gun record – seemed to descend on neighborhood gun stores to purchase the kinds of firearms the Obama Administration would most likely target with bans.

Arguably as offensive to common sense is the kind of hypocrisy that attacks the firearm but not the criminal; that is, a philosophy that would punish the gun but no the person who misuses it.

This brings us around to the curious case of Chicago's Rev. Michael Pfleger, a Catholic priest and spearhead of a movement called Clergy for Safer Streets. Father Pfleger is the man who was arrested outside of Chuck's Gun Shop in suburban Riverdale, Illinois along with Jesse Jackson, for trespass on private property. They were blocking the door to Chuck's.

Pfleger and Jackson appeared at a couple of demonstrations in the early summer of 2007 at or near Chuck's, and one of those appearances resulted in a torrent of complaints from gun owners to the Chicago Archdiocese. Pfleger ignited the controversy by suggesting that gun shop proprietor John Riggio should be "snuffed out." In street parlance, the good father was telling his audience that Riggio should be killed. Pfleger claimed ignorance, despite the fact that the term "snuff" had been associated with killing someone for many years, even in the movies and on television. Not understanding the gravity of his own remarks may be but one of Father Pfleger's shortcomings.

By remarkable coincidence, in 2004, Pfleger told co-author Workman in an interview that appeared in *Gun Week*, a newspaper published by the Second Amendment Foundation, that he started a "gun turn-in" program in memory of his adopted 17-year-old son, who had been gunned down in 1988 by an unidentified killer. But Pfleger acknowledged that he was far less interested in catching the killer and seeing justice done than he was in getting firearms out of the community. At the time, he acknowledged that hard-core criminals do not turn in their guns.

Studies have indicated that such turn-in efforts are quick to get plenty of media attention, but in a practical sense, they have not had any discernible impact on crime rates.

Admitting that he is "very, very anti-gun," Pfleger offered this remarkable observation: "I've found that people who have a gun and use it in crime don't give it up. People who basically have crime guns are people who usually hold onto their guns."

Pfleger gained more prominence for coming to the defense of Rev. Jeremiah Wright in 2008 when Wright – an African-American and military veteran – became the focus of a controversy over his recorded anti-American remarks in which he substituted "God Damn America" for "God Bless America." Wright had been then-presidential candidate Barack Hussein Obama's pastor for the past 20 years.

Pfleger's gun turn-in program had a legal snag that nobody was eager to address. Because he did not have an Illinois Firearms Owner Identification (FOID) Card, nor was he a licensed firearms dealer, Pfleger could not legally take possession of any firearm, anywhere in Illinois, much less downtown Chicago. Pfleger was ostensibly working in cooperation with the Chicago police, and at the time, a department spokesman was less-than-cooperative, actually hanging up on the author.

When it comes to gun control, Father Pfleger possibly has no equal in the pulpit. He once told his parishioners that "If you're not a law enforcement officer you should not have a gun in your house." This is essentially the priest's spin on an argument that has dated back decades; that "only cops should have guns." For a gun control proponent living in Chicago, that is hardly an argument that should be made, especially at the time he made it.

Less than a year earlier, in mid-summer 2003, Workman had publicly demanded to know – in a column published in the *Chicago Tribune* – how it was that the murder weapon used by workplace killer Salvador Tapia in the controversial Windy City Core Supply massacre on August 27, 2003, had passed through the hands of two Chicago police officers without ever having been registered under a city ordinance.

The two officers had passed away by the time Tapia showed up at the auto parts warehouse to gun down six people in what appears to have been the act of a disgruntled former employee. One of the deceased officers had purchased the murder weapon, a .380-caliber Walther PP semiautomatic pistol, from its only legal owner in 1994. For nine years, that pistol was unaccounted for legally, and author Workman made no friends among Chicago's police hierarchy when he asked, "Now, why would two Chicago cops have owned the same undocumented small-caliber handgun? For what purpose would they have wanted such a pistol? It's not approved for back-up in Chicago, and it's not legal for other Chicago residents to own an unregistered handgun. How did Tapia get his hands on it?"

One implication was that this pistol may have been a "throw down gun" to be possibly used at a crime scene to cover up the shooting of an unarmed suspect, though nobody, including author Workman, ever made that specific allegation. Another possibility is that the two deceased officers had simply wanted a pistol of some value and disregarded the city's handgun registration requirement, properly believing it to be a smoke-and-mirrors approach to crime control. No gun registration statute or local ordinance has ever prevented a criminal act. This is especially true in Chicago, which has often led the nation in homicides.

Tapia had a lengthy criminal record, though nothing approaching the magnitude of a mass killing, so he could not have legally possessed a handgun regardless of Chicago's handgun ban. It might be argued that with his record, Tapia should not have even been loose on the street. Because the two officers who had owned the pistol were both deceased, it did not appear a high priority of the police to determine just how that gun did get into Tapia's possession. Besides, Tapia had been killed in an exchange of gunfire with responding police officers.

When the Windy City Core Supply killings occurred, Chicago Mayor Richard Daley, then-Acting Police Superintendent Phil Cline and Chris McGrath, executive director of an extremist gun control group called Handgun-Free America, all declared the shooting a travesty, and an example of "what can happen when guns end up in the hands of people who should never be allowed to have them."

All three suddenly became mute when the pistol's checkered history became public knowledge. Hardly could they complain that the pistol had been funneled into the city illegally, because it had always been in the city, having been purchased legally by Milton R. Beuck in 1967. He had registered the pistol, as required by Chicago ordinance, in 1983. In the wake of the massacre, and in an obvious and horribly mismanaged attempt to shift blame for that gun being used in a crime, Beuck – then a 58-year-old homeless man – was jailed for failure to keep a record of the pistol's sale for ten years as required by law. On

September 9, 2003, Beuck was given a one-year conditional discharge on that criminal complaint by Cook County Circuit Judge Marvin Luckman.

The same hypocrisy that was vocalized by Father Pfleger and had rendered silent Mayor Daley, Supt. Cline and anti-gunner McGrath following the Windy City gun revelation may be found at the core of the gun control movement.

In his *Shotgun News* column of January 1, 2009 author Jeff Knox, a second-generation gun rights activist, reported a curious phenomenon revealed by the "Sportsman for Obama?" website. This forum, according to Knox, "noticed that thousands of visitors stopped by looking for information about Obama's position on guns and gun control on the day after the election!

"The traffic pattern leading up to the election," Knox wrote, "was pretty predictable, with increased traffic as the election grew closer. The number hovered between 700 and 1,000 until November 3 when it went up to 1,370. Then on November 4, Election Day, it peaked at 1,901. We can give those people the benefit of doubt and assume they were investigating before they voted, but then on November 5, there were 2,415 visitors – almost a 50% increase over the previous day's high. This indicates to me that there were a lot of people trying to figure out what they were in for after it was too late to do anything about it."

Knox had opened his column by observing, "The reality of the November 4 election is beginning to settle in and the more people learn about the choices they've made, the more concerned they become."

The rush to gun shops could not be merely dismissed as the manifestation of right wing gun nut paranoia because many gun shops reported that large numbers of their post-election customers were first-time gun buyers. These people had never before owned a firearm, and while it is only anecdotal evidence, among such gun purchasers were people willing to acknowledge they had cast their votes for Obama and other Democrats at the state and local level.

In our earlier book *These Dogs Don't Hunt: The Democrats' War on Guns*, we detailed the sorry history of the Democratic Party as it relates to firearms civil rights. Democrats as a whole have a dismal record on gun rights, dating back to enactment of the Black Codes in the post-Civil War South, the Sullivan Act in New York City, and more recent handgun bans, or laws that were so restrictive as to essentially constitute bans, enacted under Democrat administrations in Chicago and Washington, D.C.

What possessed voters in 2008 to believe that Old Guard Democrats may have changed their philosophy about gun rights until about five minutes after they had submitted their ballots cannot be explained. But the fact remains that this "gun rush" happened, and for weeks following the election, many firearms retailers reported that they could barely keep their shelves stocked with certain types of firearms, and the ammunition for which those guns are chambered.

At the top of the purchase list were semiautomatic rifles, the habitually misidentified "assault weapons," followed by semiautomatic handguns, followed by home-security shotguns, and on down the list.

Displaying a monumental level of social hypocrisy, many of these gun buyers demonstrated by their actions rather than any words that they had suddenly, or perhaps not so suddenly, realized that they had elected people who might just ban some types of firearms, so they "got theirs before the supply ran out." In the process, these same people essentially transformed themselves into the stereotypical gun owner they previously loved to hate; a person with little or no experience or proper training in the safe use of a firearm. They became just the type of individual against whom they might have believed gun control laws should be exercised.

With no small amount of irony, they also exhibited the kind of paranoia about potential gun bans that they had accused gun rights activists of harboring. Were it not dealing with so serious a threat to a fundamental civil right, the blinders-on social epiphany that transformed these liberal voters into worried gun owners would have been hilarious.

Yet challenge some of these same citizens to explain their vote and then balance it against their subsequent purchasing behavior, and the reaction will clearly define a sense of class distinction. "Well, *we're* different." "I'm smarter than those people." "I'm more responsible than they are."

Quite possibly the epitome of this philosophical approach is the American Hunters and Shooters Association (AHSA), founded in 2006 in an acknowledged effort to draw members away from the National Rifle Association, and to present what appeared to the general public to be a divided front on gun rights issues. AHSA is, in fact, the brainchild of Democrat party activists, and it endorsed Barack Obama for president during the primary season in March 2008.

AHSA claims to be a gun rights organization but unlike every other such group, AHSA is on record in support of issues that are on the anti-gun wish list.

For example, AHSA favors closing a mythical "gun show loophole" by requiring federal background checks on all transactions despite the fact that studies have shown that gun shows are the source of less than one percent (0.7 percent) of guns used by criminals.

The AHSA website also reports that the organization supports legislation that would regulate the ownership of modern semiautomatic sport/competition rifles chambered for the .50 BMG cartridge – dubbed "sniper rifles" by AHSA and self-admitted gun control organizations such as the Brady Campaign to Prevent Gun Violence in an effort to demonize these cumbersome firearms – the same as machine guns.

However, when asked to explain why this particular class of firearms should be heavily regulated, none of the proponents can cite any pattern of criminal behavior involving these guns. There was such a rifle reportedly recovered from the rubble of the Mount Carmel compound occupied by the Branch Davidians outside of Waco, Texas before it was burned to the ground at the end of a 53-day standoff in early 1993.

"Since the passage of the (National Firearms Act) in 1934, crimes committed with machine guns are almost nonexistent," the AHSA says on its website.

Indeed, only one crime committed by the legal owner of a machine gun has ever been reported, and that crime involved an off-duty police officer in Ohio.

When challenged to justify support for regulating .50 BMG caliber rifles AHSA, like the gun control lobbying groups, can only say it is because of the *potential* (make that the possibility) that such a gun might be used in a criminal act.

"Because of the potential for criminal misuse," AHSA contends, "the immense 'fire power' and the potential for terrorist use, AHSA believes the .50 caliber BMG sniper rifles should be regulated in the same manner as the federal government regulates machine guns under the provisions of the National Firearms Act of 1934."

By that logic, cars ought to be heavily regulated, if not outright banned, because of their already demonstrated criminal misuse by drunk drivers, car thieves, drive-by shooters, kidnappers and speeders, and they kill thousands of people every year.

There was no evidence – *none* – at the time this book was written that a single person had ever been killed with one of these rifles on American soil.

Yet AHSA would support legislation severely regulating these firearms and their owners. Why? Because they look menacing? Because someone doesn't like them? It certainly could not be because these guns are at the root of some violent crime wave in the United States, since they are not.

A gun rights organization, if it truly is one, cannot make any distinction between firearm types if they claim to support gun rights for all gun owners. Doing otherwise amounts to an exercise in class bigotry; i.e. "my gun is a *good* gun, his gun is a *bad* gun."

This strikes right at the heart of the gun control movement and the philosophy that drives it.

There are no *good* or *bad* guns. There are good and bad people who use guns, either properly or improperly, respectively. One group should not be held accountable or punished for the misbehavior of the other.

The nature of gun control laws, however, is to do exactly that: place barriers on legal gun owners. Why? Because gun control proponents have yet to devise a single mechanism that targets only criminals and punishes their behavior.

Some will argue that this is what the Brady Background Check has accomplished, but that is simply disingenuous. Criminal background checks have allegedly prevented more than a million people from buying guns at retail, but there is a caveat that nobody in the gun control movement cares to discuss. These sales are blocked, but the people attempting to buy the guns are not arrested, they merely are refused the purchase and they leave the store or gun shop. Ultimately, if they truly are intent on committing a violent criminal attack, these disqualified persons obtain firearms by some other means, typically in a street purchase, by stealing a gun or getting one from a friend or family member.

In the process, the Brady Background Check, called "NICS" (for National Instant Check System), inconveniences – sometimes for days – law-abiding citizens who have no intent to commit a violent act. The NICS system can delay the legitimate, lawful purchase of a firearm by a citizen in good standing for hours or even days, or sometimes wrongfully denied a purchase because their names match the name of some criminal. There is also the possibility that some of these purchases are delayed or denied because of a crime committed by an individual who stole someone else's identity.

As the late Dr. Martin Luther King – himself a gun owner – once observed, "A right delayed is a right denied."

Incredibly, there are gun owners who have bought into this class bigotry over the years by supporting firearms laws that do not affect the kinds of guns they personally own. This elitism surfaced dramatically in 1993 during debates on the Brady Act, which established waiting periods for handgun purchases and ultimately subjected all retail firearm purchases to the NICS check.

Initially, support for the Brady Law came from trap and skeet shooters, and precision rifle competitors, for example. Many who openly discussed the issue at the time bluntly stated that they don't own handguns and saw no reason why a person should not be subjected to scrutiny when they bought a handgun. Leap ahead five years to when the NICS system went on-line, and these same individuals suddenly learned that they, too, had to be subjected to a background check in order to purchase a skeet or trap shotgun, or a new precision target rifle. The howls of indignation were deafening, but by then, it was too late for them to protest about being "treated like criminals" just because they wanted to buy a gun.

Veteran outdoor writer Bryce Towsley, who has authored books about hunting and is an accomplished firearms authority, noted in a column that appeared in the January 5, 2009 issue of *Gun Digest the Magazine* put the issue in the perspective of Martin Niemoller, who had written about the Nazi takeover in German in the 1930s.

Paraphrasing Niemoller, Towsley wrote:

"In America, they first came for the 'assault rifles,' and I didn't speak up because I didn't own one and thought they were scary looking.

"Then they came for the semi-auto handguns and I didn't speak up because I was a bird hunter and only had shotguns.

"Then they came for the pump-action shotguns, and I didn't speak up because mine were double barrels.

"Then they came for the ammo and I didn't speak up because they didn't include birdshot.

"Then they came for my guns; and by that time there was nobody left to speak up."

Towsley cautioned gun owners: "This is no time to split our resources. We must all stick together and protect the rights and interest of all gun owners."

That appeal would fall on deaf ears at AHSA headquarters.

It would also gain little traction with gun control proponents in the media. Some, like Ken Schram at Seattle, Washington's KOMO Radio – a co-host on *The Commentators*, a point-counterpoint midday talk show – have long advocated written testing for anyone wanting to purchase a handgun.

The Civil Rights movement that arose in the 1950s and 1960s went after so-called literacy tests or competency tests that had been used to prevent black citizens from voting, thus denying those citizens their voting rights.

What is different between requiring a written test to vote and requiring a written test to exercise another constitutionally-protected civil right, the right to keep and bear arms? We are not discussing guns, we are discussing the exercise of a civil right. Is one civil right more or less important than another? Evidently so among gun control proponents.

This was precisely the issue raised by author Workman in an opinion piece published by various newspapers in early 2009 regarding Illinois Congressman Bobby Rush's H.R. 45, a bill that would require licensing and registration of handgun owners. Under Rush's bill, gun owners would initially have to register new handguns, but two years after enactment, they would be required to register all of their firearms, and repeat the process every few years, with fees that would be prohibitive for owners of multiple firearms.

Most insidious of all, in the author's opinion, was that in order to own a firearm, each citizen would first have to pass a test demonstrating their knowledge of laws and firearms safety. Workman properly compared this tenet to the literacy tests that denied black citizens their voting rights from the 1890s through the early 1960s in the Deep South.

In his opinion piece, Workman noted that "One should not be required to obtain a license or pass a government-administered test in order to exercise any constitutionally-protected civil right. If the Civil Rights movement of the 1950s and 1960s taught us anything, it is that all civil rights are sacred, one is no less important than another, and all of them are worth defending...

"Congressman Rush would demote the Second Amendment right to the rank of a privilege that can be regulated by government," Workman added. "He is, after all, from Chicago, home of a Draconian gun ban law that gun control extremists consider 'reasonable.' He would make the entire country Chicago, and while that may square with anti-gun demagogues like Mayor Richard Daley, it will not pass muster in places like Missoula, Mont., Cheyenne, Wyo., Boise, Idaho, Flagstaff, Ariz., Spokane, Wash., or just about anyplace else west of the Mississippi River or south of the Ohio River.

"Perhaps he would like to see African-American citizens face this new literacy test at the hands of some aging bureaucrat who remembers the 'good old days' when his grand-pappy was a Grand Dragon in the Klan and everybody in the county knew it," the author continued. "Suddenly, if you're black, this written gun safety test doesn't sound so hot, does it?

"Each of us has a stake in America," Workman concluded, "and it requires that we zealously protect everyone else's civil rights as we guard our own. The Bill of Rights is an all-or-nothing package, not a smorgasbord from which to select the rights we defend and those we dump in the trash. If Congressman Rush can't understand that, then perhaps it is time for competency tests for politicians."

Still, gun ban proponents persist in their argument that gun owners should be licensed, contending that we license people to drive automobiles.

Driving is a privilege in the United States, not a constitutionally-protected civil right. By putting forth this rather specious argument, gun control activists perhaps unintentionally acknowledge that they do not believe owning a firearm is a right, but only a privilege that should be tightly regulated, perhaps more tightly than owning and driving a car. It might just be that some of these individuals simply do not know the difference between a privilege and a right. (It also opens up licensing proponents to the challenge that since driver's licenses are recognized in all 50 states, a gun license should thus also be recognized. The reaction to that argument is universally negative from the gun control camp.)

Even former North Carolina senator and, for a time, Democratic presidential candidate John Edwards once acknowledged during an interview that, in his opinion, owning a handgun should be a privilege.

What these anecdotes illustrate is that there exists a cultural chasm in America dividing the Right and Left, and a key component of that great divide is gun ownership and how it is viewed. Yet, the gun debate cannot always be easily passed off as a mere dispute between liberals who hate guns and conservatives who like guns. This debate all-too-frequently transcends philosophical differences and descends to the level of class separation – call it class bigotry if you will – as addressed earlier in this chapter.

There are many social liberals who own guns, lots of guns. Perhaps thinking of themselves as a privileged class, it is not unusual to find these same people, whether they are Hollywood producers or actors, politicians or socialites, supporting gun control measures. The why of this issue is not easily explained, and one should not simply categorize such citizens as hypocrites, though their actions certain suggest hypocrisy is a part of the equation.

On another level, these privileged individuals frequently have hired security guards and live in gated communities or estates. They lose perspective regarding the average person's rights, and concerns about crime and personal safety are far from being a priority, as their status has provided at least a partial solution.

In the process, something else has been lost, and that is the perspective that government was established to serve rather than rule, and this brings us back around to the ACLU, and what should be its role in defending and protecting all civil rights, not just those it approves of as an organization. If the ACLU can defend American Nazis marching through the Jewish neighborhood in Skokie, Illinois, then it should also be pressing forward to defend the rights of firearms owners against onerous federal, state and local laws that have systematically tightened down on those rights that millions of law-abiding Americans hold so dear.

Was it not the ACLU that declared on its website, "Our constitution is meant to safeguard against government abuses of power?"

What else but an abuse of power could it be called when a legislature or the Congress passes legislation that outlaws certain types of firearms, and adds criminal penalties for their possession, even though someone who may have owned one of these suddenly contraband guns has never harmed a soul?

What else but an abuse of power, under color of law, is the act of arbitrary firearms confiscation in the wake of a natural disaster – as was the case following Hurricane Katrina – when citizens were expected to fend for themselves because there was no law enforcement and instead of law and order, the was anarchy?

The ACLU was nowhere to be found, and in its stead, the National Rifle Association and Second Amendment Foundation were compelled to seek federal court intervention in that gun seizure, which occurred under a Democrat New Orleans mayor and Democrat Louisiana governor. Citizens whose firearms were taken, often at gunpoint, were treated like criminals for no other reason than that they were armed and trying to protect what little they had left in the wake of the giant storm.

Those firearms were taken without warrant or probable cause, simply on the order of a mayor and police chief. The ACLU should have been screaming, but it was silent. No public official, police administrator or individual officer has ever been held accountable for a single illegal seizure.

So much for the ACLU's claim that it "works to reform the criminal justice system and make the promise of fair treatment a reality for all people."

Fair treatment unless those people happen to be gun owners.

CHAPTER 6

Right to Carry Hysteria

Opposition to the exercise of a constitutionally-protected civil right can assume many guises and take many approaches, not the least of which is the incessant hysteria over so-called "right-to-carry" statutes that have been adopted in a majority of states.

As we discussed in Chapter Four, there are mounting attacks on right-to-carry statutes, primarily by anti-gun municipal politicians who dislike not having the authority to regulate one more aspect of daily life for the citizens they are supposed to serve. Seattle, Washington Mayor Greg Nickels did not invent the movement to stifle concealed carry, though he has become one of its leading proponents.

There are at least 39 states where these laws require local police chiefs and sheriffs to issue concealed pistol licenses or carry permits to any law-abiding citizen who passes a background check and fulfills any other requirement. That is to say these police officials cannot, under virtually any circumstance, simply decide not to issue a carry permit to a citizen solely on the grounds of "discretion." The reason these laws were passed is because far too many local law enforcement officials were exercising their discretion in a wholly arbitrary and capricious manner, issuing only to friends, political supporters and/or the well-connected.

Of everyone else, these police officials would require a demonstrated "need" to have a gun permit, and in no case would there ever be a reason to meet the never-defined standard. Personal protection is not a sufficient need; in-store security late at night does not meet the "need standard."

The battle to prevent such laws from passing has brought out the best, or the worst depending upon perspective, in the opponents. They have unleashed tirades against such statutes, predicting all variety of calamities as a result, from gun battles over minor traffic mishaps to wholesale slaughter of innocents, and an increase in the number of police officer slayings.

A text book example of this alarmist rhetoric would be the argument against concealed carry legislation under consideration in Kansas in 2004. At the time, then-Democrat Gov. Kathleen Sebelius had claimed to support concealed carry, but only for retired police officers, as though they were somehow more entitled to self-defense than other citizens. She ultimately vetoed legislation that passed that year, but two years later, her veto of another bill was overridden and concealed carry became the law.

Quoted in the *Topeka Capital Journal* of March 27, 2004, State Senator Christine Downey, a Democrat from the town of Inman, predicted that allowing Kansas residents to carry concealed handguns would result in "collateral damage."

"By adding more guns to this state," Downey predicted, "we're going to have more suicides, we're going to have more accidental shootings – particularly of children – and we're going to have domestic violence incidents that end in more murders and more injuries than we have now."

This was a variation of the all-encompassing "guns cause mayhem" argument that also surfaced in Wisconsin when that state's legislature was debating a concealed carry bill. State Representative Spencer Black, a Madison Democrat, was quoted by *The Daily Cardinal*, the University of Wisconsin's student newspaper, asserting, "What would now be a bar fight, with a little shoving, might escalate into a shooting incident."

In 2004, Kansas reported 122 homicides statewide. The following year, that number dropped to 101, bounced back to 127 in 2006 – the year that Kansas finally adopted a concealed carry statute, the Personal & Family Protection Act – and fell again to 107 in 2007, the year that the law took effect. What these figures demonstrate is that even with adoption of a concealed carry law, homicide rates remained essentially the same, and some might suggest the number dropped when Kansans began carrying concealed handguns.

None of these doomsday scenarios ever materialized, anywhere. For example, writing in *U.S. News & World Report* on March 28, 2006, Michael Barone discussed the hysteria that preceded passage of the Kansas legislation.

"Governor Sebelius," Barone noted, "expressed some of the concerns that concealed-carry weapons opponents have often voiced (I shared them myself, when Florida became the first state to pass such a law in 1987): that there would be shootouts in the streets, that road rage would escalate into gunshot deaths.

"The experience of states with concealed-carry weapons laws seems to have proved that these concerns are unwarranted," Barone acknowledged. "Ordinary law-abiding citizens, it seems, behave responsibly when they carry guns, just as they do in other respects. Michigan Gov. Jennifer Granholm opposed that state's concealed-carry law when it was passed in 2001 (she was attorney general at the time) but has since said that fears about it had not been justified."

In early 2008, the *Detroit Free Press* reported that after six years in effect, Michigan's reformed concealed carry statute had cost fewer lives than before the law changed. Homicides and suicides with firearms had declined. Reporter Dawson Bell noted that in the years since Michigan lawmakers passed right-to-carry legislation, "The incidence of violent crime…has been, on average, below the rate of the previous six years. The overall incidence of death from firearms, including suicide and accidents, has also declined."

Wayne LaPierre, executive vice president of the National Rifle Association, also noted in an Opposing Viewpoint that appeared in the December 17, 2007 edition of *USA Today* that concealed carry laws did not have the impact that newspapers, including *USA Today*, had forecast.

"While USA TODAY predicted mayhem that never materialized," LaPierre wrote, "right-to-carry laws have spread from 15 to 40 states since 1991.

"Statistics can't console grieving families, but might be more useful than defeatist editorials in developing public firearms policy.

"Our analysis of FBI crime data shows that in 2006, compared with the rest of the country, states with right-to-carry had overall average violent crime rates 26% lower," he added. "Critics argue that right-to-carry will produce 'too many' armed citizens, but in the same breath they say that if a crime occurs, there'll be 'too few' armed citizens to be useful. The fact is, some armed citizens are always better than none."

Of course, one can dismiss LaPierre's remarks as being those of an agenda-driven lobbyist, but the same can hardly be said of Barone or Bell. However, all three appear to have arrived at the same conclusion.

A rapidly-expanding college-age group called Students for Concealed Carry on Campus (SCCC) also found some interesting observations from officials in several states where concealed carry statutes had been hotly debated. There are hardly the kinds of public statements from police and government officials that gun control hysterics prefer to read or hear because they refute the rhetoric.

For example, Glenn White, president of the Dallas Police Association, told the *Dallas Morning News* in December 1997 that, "I lobbied against the law in 1993 and 1995 because I thought it would lead to wholesale armed conflict. That hasn't happened. All the horror stories I thought would come to pass didn't happen. No bogeyman. I think it's worked out well, and that says good things about the citizens who have permits. I'm a convert."

In that same article, Harris County District Attorney John Holmes acknowledged, "I ... [felt] that such legislation present[ed] a clear and present danger to law-abiding citizens by placing more handguns on our streets. Boy was I wrong. Our experience in Harris County, and indeed statewide, has proven my fears absolutely groundless."

In Virginia, where concealed carry was also strongly resisted, Fairfax County Police Major Bill Brown told the *Alexandria Journal* in July 1997, "Some of the public safety concerns which we imagined or anticipated a couple of years ago, to our pleasant surprise, have been unfounded or mitigated."

Arlington County Police Detective Paul Larson was also quoted in that same newspaper, admitting, "I was wrong. But I'm glad to say I was wrong."

And in North Carolina, Charlotte-Mecklenburg Police Chief Dennis Nowicki told *The News and Observer* in November 1997 that "The concerns I had - with more guns on the street, folks may be more apt to square off against one another with weapons - we haven't experienced that."

Perhaps the most telling information came from the National Law Enforcement Officers Memorial Fund, which noted that 2008 saw the lowest number of police officer slayings in more than 50 years. Less than 45 officers nationwide were killed in the line of duty by gunfire, an accomplishment that should not have occurred with the proliferation of concealed carry laws, if one believed the gun prohibitionists.

This occurred at a time when gun ownership had skyrocketed during the final two months of the year as a result of the national elections that put Barack Obama in the White House and a strong Democrat majority in charge on Capitol Hill. It happened after twelve months of steady increases in the number of applications for concealed carry permits, resulting in more than five million American citizens who were licensed to carry.

There were no huge body counts, and the multiple-victim shootings that did occur were typically found to be the handiwork of people who were carrying illegally, either without a permit or because their criminal records prevented them from obtaining a permit, much less having a firearm in their possession. Such individuals historically violate gun laws out of habit, and to associate their misbehavior with the conduct of legally-armed citizens is misdirected.

However, being wrong never stops gun control lobbyists. For whatever reason, firearms prohibitionists cling to the position that more firearms in private hands will lead to violence and even anarchy.

Take, for example, the opinion piece authored by California Sen. Dianne Feinstein, one of the nation's leading gun control advocates, in the December 29, 2008 edition of the *San Francisco Chronicle*. In her tirade against the change in national park rules in late 2008 to allow licensed concealed carry in national parks, Feinstein regurgitated every argument that had been prominently made by the anti-gun lobby in the months leading up to the change in rules.

Here's what she predicted:

"Allowing loaded and accessible weapons in our national parks will create a dangerous environment for the millions of Americans and tourists from around the world who visit our national parks every year.

These park visitors expect a safe and enjoyable experience - not loaded guns and stray bullets.

"Poaching will increase in our national parks, upsetting the delicate balance between park visitors and wildlife.

"It will create a confusing patchwork of regulation that will be impossible to enforce. That's because some parks, like Death Valley National Park, cross state lines. California prohibits concealed weapons in its state parks. Nevada does not. Which state's law will apply at Death Valley?

"The new regulation itself is vague and confusing because it permits state law on gun possession to determine whether guns are allowed in national parks. But many states - including California - generally allow the carrying of concealed weapons with a permit, but prohibit their possession in state parks. The new regulation isn't clear on which state law applies."

There is no evidence anywhere that the new firearms regulation would lead to that kind of scenario in the national parks and national wildlife refuges, and Sen. Feinstein knows it. But Feinstein, like other gun control absolutists, was not trying to be factual; she was attempting to sway an audience by misleading them, creating the false impression that the public has something to fear from legally-armed fellow citizens.

It is ironic that Feinstein chose to complain about a potential "confusing patchwork of regulation that will be impossible to enforce," when that is exactly the kind of scenario frequently supported by gun control advocates, when it conveniently fits their political strategy of the moment. Where the gun control lobby once advocated national firearms laws, they now have shifted to "local control," which translates to allowing municipal governments determine their own gun ordinances.

No matter that such a patchwork of ordinances might allow for a citizen to carry a firearm in one city, but soon as that individual crosses a municipal boundary, which may be a street, or a river, or just an imaginary line across the landscape, he could be in violation. Conviction for such violations would likely carry with it the loss of a carry permit, perhaps forever, and confiscation of the firearm. Such a conviction might also disqualify the gun owner from every owning a firearm of any kind.

As if coming to Feinstein's rescue, the Brady Campaign on December 30, 2008 filed a lawsuit in U.S. District Court for the District of Columbia, seeking an injunction against the rule change.

In its press release announcing the lawsuit, the Brady Campaign declared, "Numerous studies have confirmed that concealed carrying of firearms does not reduce crime and, if anything, leads to increased violent crime. Experience in states that have allowed concealed carrying of firearms has shown that thousands of dangerous people are able to get licenses. In Florida, for example, more than 4,200 licenses were revoked because many of these licensees committed a crime. Since becoming the first state to allow the concealed carrying of firearms in 1987, Florida consistently has had one of the highest rates of violent crime in the nation. Florida has been ranked as the state with the highest annual violent crime rate more often than any other state in the last two decades."

Once again, the Brady Campaign was being disingenuous in its remarks.

A check with the Florida Division of Licensing revealed that the revocations alluded to by the Brady Campaign occurred over a 21-year period, amounting to slightly more than 214 revocations per year, a remarkably low number (if one were to accept the Brady Campaign's remarks at face value) considering that the state had issued more than 1.4 *million* concealed carry permits in that period.

The Brady Campaign would have the public believe that all of those revocations to which it alluded had something to do with firearms, but again, the Division of Licensing data showed only 166 of those revocations was for a crime involving a firearm. The remaining revocations were for other reasons, including some other type of crime committed after the permit had been issued. More than 500 of those permits had been reinstated, another fact that the Brady Campaign deliberately overlooked.

Written to link Florida's rising crime rate with the growing number of legally-armed citizens in the Sunshine State is also deliberately deceptive. These crimes about which the gun control lobby laments are not being committed by law-abiding armed Florida residents, who have – as noted above – a stunningly low involvement in serious crimes.

According to Wikipedia, which discussed this issue, "Permit holders are a remarkably law-abiding subclass of the population." In addition to discussing Florida's concealed carry history, Wikipedia also noted that North Carolina had reported only 0.2 percent of its more than 263,000 licenses had been revoked from licensees in the ten years since the concealed carry statute was adopted, and data had been maintained.

Washington, D.C.'s congressional delegate, Liberal Democrat Eleanor Holmes Norton, pushed the anti-carry hysteria level higher in the days leading up to the inauguration of Barack Obama as president. Quoted by *The Hill*, Norton offered the preposterous supposition that the national park rule change would leave citizens convinced they could carry handguns in the District of Columbia for the January 20, 2009 inaugural events.

Norton knew that wasn't true, just as she knew in mid-2008 when the U.S. Supreme Court handed down its landmark Second Amendment ruling in the case of *District of Columbia v. Dick Anthony Heller* that the city would not suddenly allow concealed or open carry of firearms. Yet there she was, telling the newspaper, "It is truly frightening to think of what this (parks rule change) could mean coming just a couple of weeks before the inauguration."

Paul Helmke, president of the Brady Campaign, echoed Norton's paranoia about armed citizens attending the Obama inauguration, telling *The Hill*, "My concern is that there has been some publicity about this whole guns in the parks thing and some of the 4 million people coming in from all over the country (may) think that just because they have a concealed carry permit in their home state, that it gives them the right to come to the nation's capital and carry (a gun)."

Apparently, the newspaper did not care to challenge this nonsense, instead allowing Helmke to plant the subliminal notion that armed citizens are not bright enough to realize the difference between carrying a concealed firearm into a national park, and bringing one into the nation's capital, to attend a presidential inauguration.

Nowhere has the opposition to concealed carry been more dramatic than in debates about allowing legally-licensed adults – both students and teachers – on college and university campuses to carry defensive firearms. This controversy erupted on the day after the horrific Virginia Tech massacre of April 16, 2007. That was the day that Students for Concealed Carry on Campus was formed and within four months, there were more than 60 chapters on college and university campuses nationwide.

SCCC members are all college students, and they argue that allowing armed students and teachers on campus would thwart or reduce the carnage in the event another campus shooting erupted. Only legally-licensed students – meaning that students age 21 or over in most states – and staff would be allowed to carry as they might carry concealed handguns off campus.

Opposition to the proposal was swift and shrill. The Brady Campaign to Prevent Gun Violence quickly put together arguments against the idea and accused SCCC of being financed by the firearms industry. SCCC leaders quickly challenged the Brady Campaign to prove the allegation, and also promised to debate the organization on any campus in the country.

Instead, the Brady Campaign issued a report titled *No Gun Left Behind: The Gun Lobby's Campaign to Push Guns Into Colleges and Schools*. In their report, the Brady Campaign portrayed college students as an unstable lot: "Drugs and alcohol use, plus suicide and mental health issues, all peak for people 18-24. Let's not ad guns into that volatile mix."

On their website, the Brady Campaign frantically alleged that if state legislatures passed laws to prevent colleges and universities from banning licensed concealed carry on their campuses, "it would mean 18-year-old kids could carry handguns to class, and kids even younger than 18 could possess AK-47 assault rifles with high-capacity magazines on campus."

This is a deliberately inflammatory falsehood, yet nobody in the media questioned the Brady Campaign about the assertion. SCCC leaders were aghast at the vilification unleashed by the anti-gun lobbying group, which stereotyped college undergraduates as being in their "peak years for engaging in gun crimes, abusing drugs and alcohol, attempting suicide, and having other mental health problems."

"A binge-drinking, drug abusing student is dangerous enough," the Brady Campaign hysterically declared, "let's not give him or her a gun."

The Brady Campaign, relying on a study by the National Center on Addiction and Substance Abuse (CASA) at Columbia University, and a survey of college students that appeared in the *Journal of American College Health* (Vol. 51, No. 2), alleged that "Nearly half of America's full-time college students abuse drugs or binge drink at least once a month. For college gun owners, the rate of binge-drinking is even higher – two-thirds."

Another argument was that "Guns stolen from homes and cars fuel crime. College dorm rooms, by comparison, would be even easier targets for gun thieves."

What the Brady Campaign did not discuss, and what W. Scott Lewis with SCCC *did* reveal on his organization's website, is that the handful of college and university campuses that do allow concealed carry have experienced no shootings or mishaps.

In an article headlined "Will Allowing Concealed Carry on College Campuses Lead to More Violence," Lewis noted, "At least eleven U.S. colleges (all nine public colleges in the state of Utah, Colorado State University, and Blue Ridge Community College in Weyers Cave, VA) have, for a combined total of more than seventy semesters, allowed concealed carry on campus, without a single resulting incident of gun violence, without a single gun accident, and without a single gun theft."

Perhaps the proverbial "bottom line" in this debate is the viewpoint offered by Wisconsin State Rep. Terese Berceau, a Madison Democrat, during the debate over that state's failed attempt to pass a concealed carry statute. Wisconsin, at the time this book was written, was one of only two states in the country that did not have some kind of provision for concealed carry, the other being Illinois.

Her principle objection was – as are the arguments from so many other concealed carry opponents – based on emotion rather than statistics or the experiences of other states. Quoted by *The Daily Cardinal*, the student newspaper at the University of Wisconsin – Madison, Berceau suggested that making concealed carry legal would make Madison residents nervous.

"I just don't see any need to have the average citizen going around armed," she stated.

That really appears to be the core of the argument. Opponents of concealed carry simply do not like the idea of private citizens driving or walking around armed for their personal safety.

One can line up clinical psychologists and try to explain this phenomenon, but as discussed in Chapter One, the opposition to concealed carry, and the hysteria that is fomented to drive that opposition, may be no more complicated than the simple explanation that those who are against concealed carry dislike guns in general.

There might also be a sentiment against self-reliance that is a natural component of arming for self-defense. For many Americans who have grown up in an urban environment where government and social services are more available, the notion of doing something on one's own, particularly defending one's self or family against criminal attack, is so foreign as to be repugnant.

One of the nation's leading home alarm companies introduced a series of commercials in 2008 that portrayed homeowners – typically cast as women – who were saved from home invasion by a screeching alarm. This alarm would be set off by some hooded or dark-clad figure breaking through a door or window. Immediately, the telephone would ring and the handsome, serious-looking actor portraying the alarm company employee would identify himself, ask if everything is alright, and then tell the frightened subscriber, "I'm sending help right now!"

Average citizens might not understand the subliminal message here, which is that the homeowner needs an alarm company to watch over him or her, and also to send the police. For private citizens who have convinced themselves that they are not capable of dialing 9-1-1 on their own, or defending themselves at home against a violent intruder, the alarm company advertisement may offer some peace of mind.

The advertisement offered no advice at all on what course of action, and what preventive measures one might take away from home, and away from the debatable protection of the alarm system. Further, today's serious home invaders are a sometimes crafty bunch, capable of disarming such alarm systems. No advice on what to do there, either.

Likewise, stern police officials as a matter of policy after every self-defense shooting are quick to tell reporters that "We never recommend taking direct action, but instead call the police and let us handle (the crisis)."

Gone from the debate is the perfectly legitimate argument that private citizens under immediate and unavoidable attack do not have the luxury of alarm company guardian angels, or the time it takes to call 9-1-1 and wait for an operator to pick up the call, then alert the dispatcher who then alerts a patrol officer there is a problem. By the time the police arrive, the crime is typically concluded, the perpetrator has left the scene and there is a victim who, if he or she is lucky, is still alive to provide the details of the rape, robbery, physical assault, mass shooting, attempted murder or attempted kidnapping, carjacking or whatever other crime has just occurred.

Heaven forbid that the intended victim would draw a legally-concealed handgun and drop a criminal in his tracks.

This goes against the philosophy of Brian J. Siebel, a senior attorney with the Brady Center and author of the aforementioned *No Gun Left Behind: The Gun Lobby's Campaign to Push Guns Into Colleges and Schools*. Writing an opinion piece for the Roanoke, Virginia *Times* on July 1, 2007, Siebel – arguing against a proposal to allow armed students and faculty on Nevada campuses – wrote, "If the Nevada System of Higher Education is serious about enhancing campus security, more resources should be dedicated to hiring more law enforcement, better campus communication systems, implementing campus security plans and identifying troubled students before tragedy strikes. Leave security and law enforcement to those with the proper experience and thorough training."

And what are you supposed to do while waiting for the police to arrive? Opponents of concealed carry never seem to have the answer to that question. What they offer instead are contentions, often unsupported by facts, that concealed carry will contribute to street crime and violence, rather than deter it.

That is what the Brady Campaign asserted in its press release announcing the lawsuit against concealed carry in national parks. Their claim that "Numerous studies have confirmed that concealed carrying of firearms does not reduce crime and, if anything, leads to increased violent crime," was not backed up by any documentation.

Conversely, research that demonstrated quite the opposite has become a cornerstone of gun rights arguments for many years. The

1998 book *More Guns = Less Crime* by John Lott and David Mustard studied crime data from every county in the United States over a multi-year period, and determined that passage of concealed carry laws combined with general widespread gun ownership correlated with reductions in violent crime, while property crimes went up.

The Lott-Mustard research was bitterly attacked by anti-gun researchers, but the conclusions offered by the two academics has borne up well under scrutiny. On the other hand, areas where strict gun laws are enforced have some of the highest crime statistics in the nation. Chicago, New York City, Washington, D.C., Milwaukee and other enclaves of the gun control culture are relatively awash in blood when compared to communities where a large percentage of the population is armed.

Quoted by Wikipedia, attorney Don Kates – himself an authority on firearms legislation and its effects – noted, "Unfortunately, an almost perfect inverse correlation exists between those who are affected by gun laws, particularly bans, and those whom enforcement should affect. Those easiest to disarm are the responsible and law abiding citizens whose guns represent no meaningful social problem. Irresponsible and criminal owners, whose gun possession creates or exacerbates so many social ills, are the ones most difficult to disarm."

Another revelation – the kind that the gun control lobby despises – came from research conducted by Brandon Centerwall at the University of Washington in Seattle. As reported by Wikipedia in its lengthy discussion of concealed carry in the United States, "Centerwall prepared a study comparing homicide rates between Canada and the U.S., as the two countries are very similar, yet have different handgun ownership rates. He reported 'Major differences in the prevalence of handguns have not resulted in differing total criminal homicide rates in Canadian provinces and adjoining US states.' In his conclusions he published the following admonition: 'If you are surprised by my findings, so are we. We did not begin this research with any intent to 'exonerate' handguns, but there it is – a negative finding, to be sure, but a negative finding is nevertheless a positive contribution. It directs us where NOT to aim public health resources'."

CHAPTER 7

The Process of Demonization

Firearms owners are the only remaining social group in America against whom it is perfectly acceptable to practice social bigotry, often to the extreme. They are often demonized as are the firearms they own, by the repeated use of carefully selected rhetoric, or perhaps not-so-carefully selected, but still excusable since it is used to vilify gun owners.

The Kennedy generation, those who witnessed both the assassinations of President John F. Kennedy and his brother, Senator Robert F. Kennedy, should still recall then-president Lyndon Baines Johnson declaring, "We must stop this insane traffic in guns!"

It did not matter to Johnson that both killings appeared to be the work of single assassins (though one will still encounter devoted arguments that the murder of John Kennedy was a conspiracy, and that Sirhan Sirhan was not the only gunman in the hotel that night when Robert was slain), and that even experts agree that it is virtually impossible to stop lone gunmen from doing whatever they intend.

But after those murders, and the killing of Dr. Martin Luther King, Congress passed the Gun Control Act of 1968, a federal statute that has spawned many other laws, all of which tend to treat all firearms buyers as potential criminals, guilty until proven innocent via background checks and waiting periods.

The "waiting period" has been particularly onerous because its basic concept is that it gives the potential gun buyer time to "cool off." Alternately called a "cooling-off period," the reason this was established in law was because of alleged incidents in which people argued, one went out and bought a gun, came back and killed the other.

The "cooling-off period" presumes that every gun purchaser is angry and intends to kill another person.

Adopted ostensibly to prevent heat-of-the-moment killings, waiting periods have proven rather ineffective. For example, would-be Ronald Reagan assassin John Hinckley, Jr. passed a waiting period and then kept the .22-caliber revolver he used to shoot Reagan, Press Secretary James Brady (for whom the Brady Campaign to Prevent Gun Violence is named), a Secret Service agent and a Washington, D.C. police officer for several months before actually committing the crime.

Colin Ferguson, the racist gunman who shot several people on a Long Island commuter train, traveled to California to buy the gun eight months before he committed the crime. Ferguson underwent the state's 15-day waiting period to legally obtain the 9mm pistol he used. Among his victims was Dennis McCarthy, husband of Carolyn McCarthy, who went on to run for Congress as a stiff gun control proponent, and who remains there today as one of Capitol Hill's most ardent gun rights foes.

Further infringements on the right to keep and bear arms followed enactment of the 1968 Gun Control Act at the state level, in California, for example, where a deliberately intimidating display of firearms by members of the Black Panthers in May 1967 at the capitol in Sacramento led that state's legislature to pass legislation against open carry of firearms.

Two years later, Washington's Legislature passed a statute in reaction to the California demonstration, but instead of banning open carry outright – which they cannot do in Washington due to the state's constitutional right to bear arms provision – the law prevents carrying guns or other weapons "in a manner, under circumstances, and at a time and place that either manifests an intent to intimidate another or that warrants alarm for the safety of other persons."

This oddball statute, the only one like it in America, has been narrowed in its scope by at least two Washington Appellate Court rulings, but the law has yet to be completely struck down. The mere existence of the statute has empowered anti-gunners to report armed citizens to police on the flimsy grounds that the appearance of a firearm carried peaceably is still alarming to them.

When Sarah Brady, the public face of the Brady Campaign to Prevent Gun Violence, can put her name on the organization's fund-raising propaganda and hysterically declare that "We need to get these 'killing machines' off our streets" as she alludes to semiautomatic firearms, that is demonization. It is designed to elicit fear and loathing of a firearm instead of a criminal who may misuse that firearm.

Add to this the Brady campaign's claim that perfectly-legal private sales of firearms, often between friends, gun club members or relatives amounts to "giving criminals and terrorists remarkably easy and undetectable access to weapons." This argument was made in a document that the gun control lobbying group submitted to the incoming Obama administration in late 2008. This 16-page document amounted to a wish list of proposed restrictions on gun owners titled *Gun Violence In America.*

In that document, the Brady Campaign suggested that "gun companies…arm criminals." They invent a new and alarmist term, the "terror gap," as a means of promoting legislation that would give the United States Attorney General the discretionary authority to block firearms sales to someone who is a "suspected terrorist" when that individual – who may not be guilty of anything – has committed no crime.

This discretionary authority could be used against anyone who has suddenly found himself or herself on a law enforcement "watch list." There are cases of public figures and public officials who have ended up on such watch lists and have no idea how or why their names were put on those lists. More alarming is the fact that nobody has yet explained how one gets his or her name off of such a list.

Social demonization takes many forms, and it represents the insidious nature of the bigotry unleashed against gun owners or anyone who espouses support for firearm ownership or the shooting sports. This campaign is not aimed at merely pressing an agenda, but for the more sinister purpose of silencing the gun owners whose firearms civil rights are being eroded. For some gun banners, "quieting" the opposition takes a distant second place to silencing it altogether.

From the depiction of gun owners as pot-bellied buffoons by anti-gun editorial cartoonists to the use of vituperative headlines and remarks in opinion pieces that appear in newspapers and magazines, law-abiding firearms owners have become the public whipping boys for all of the criminals who misuse guns, and all of the public officials who seem unable or unwilling to stop them.

Perhaps no better proof that this bigotry exists and that it is not restricted by gender, fact or even good taste was the speech delivered by black Florida Congressman Alcee Hastings during the 2008 presidential campaign when he addressed a group of Jewish and African-American Democrats on September 24. His remarks were aimed at vice presidential candidate Sarah Palin, the conservative governor of Alaska, whom had become the primary target of media scorn and ridicule in a campaign that revealed just how biased toward Democrats the nation's press corps had become.

"If Sarah Palin isn't enough of a reason for you to get over whatever your problem is with Barack Obama, then you damn well had better pay attention," Hastings commented. "Anybody toting guns and stripping moose don't care too much about what they do with Jews and blacks. So, you just think this through."

Astonishingly, the audience of blacks and Jews laughed and applauded energetically. Nobody called Congressman Hastings, a black man, on the proverbial carpet over his deplorable remark.

Palin, of course, had emerged on the national scene only weeks before as Republican John McCain's running mate, and the press immediately went on the attack. A conservative outdoorswoman who had climbed to the office of governor in Alaska after having served as mayor of Wasilla, occupying a seat on the state's energy board until she quit that post in protest over cronyism, and gotten her start as a community activist after having been a female sports reporter for an Anchorage television station – all the kinds of things that would win accolades for a liberal woman – perhaps Palin's biggest offense was that she candidly acknowledged that she is a Life Member of the National Rifle Association.

The Left's attacks on Palin, and the brutal scrutiny to which she was subjected by a press corps that was all but endorsing Barack Hussein Obama, demonstrated the lengths to which gun rights opponents will go to marginalize and ultimately destroy anyone who professes support for Second Amendment rights. It is an effort to deny someone like Palin the stage, to prevent her from being heard, and subsequently to prevent the millions of citizens whose sentiments she represents from being heard as well.

What happened to Sarah Palin has been happening to America's gun owners for many years. The Palin case simply added a new perspective to this campaign of bigotry, which those who are doing it will deny or dismiss as their right to criticize that which they do not like.

Gun rights activists such as blogger and novelist Mike Vanderboegh of Alabama have noted how gun control advocates have carefully described their demands for ever-increasing restrictions on gun rights as "common sense" proposals. Laws that subject firearms owners to degrees of scrutiny far beyond that which would be tolerated by First Amendment advocates are called "reasonable."

The subliminal message here is that anyone opposing these statutes is both unreasonable and lacking in common sense.

Semiautomatic firearms have been successfully labeled "assault weapons" though the correct definition of such a weapon is that it may be made to fire either full- or semi-automatic; that is, a flip of a lever allows the user to fire several shots with one squeeze of the trigger, or fire a single round each time the trigger is pressed.

A true semiautomatic rifle wrongly described as an "assault weapon" functions no differently than guns that have been used by hunters and target shooters across the country for more than 100 years.

Hunting and sporting rifles equipped with telescopic sights have suddenly become "sniper rifles." As noted earlier, one type of firearm specifically singled out for this demonization is the .50-caliber, which historically has not been used in criminal activities.

Some time ago, the Violence Policy Center assembled a lengthy list of cases in which .50-caliber rifles allegedly were involved. A careful reading of this list shows that the overwhelming majority of the 29 cases mentioned involved rifles that were recovered in connection with searches and raids. They simply happened to be "recovered evidence," without having ever been fired. By comparison, nobody has suggested that automobiles recovered in these same investigations are somehow the evil tools of criminals or terrorists.

Who can forget the term "cop-killer bullets?" Now a part of the American lexicon, the term was something of an invention by gun control extremists who were trying to ban virtually every caliber of centerfire rifle ammunition in the United States. The reason such ammunition would have been banned, had not the National Rifle

Association and other gun rights groups intervened, is that they all fire bullets at velocities capable of penetrating the soft body armor typically worn by police officers today. Those so-called "bullet-proof vests" are designed from tightly-woven materials that are layered in such a way as to stop *most* (but not all) pistol bullets.

The ultimate goal was to ban ammunition, thus rendering every hunting rifle in America useless, which is precisely what gun prohibitionists want. Of course these gun control advocates knew from the outset that this ban on so-called "cop-killer bullets" would eliminate hunting ammunition. They also knew *that no police officer in the United States had ever been killed with an actual armor-piercing bullet while wearing a bullet-resistant vest.* They did not care. This was an effort to ban ammunition, and they were determined to succeed.

The press, as noted in an earlier chapter, has been a willing ally in this campaign of demonization. How many times, for example, have news reports gasped about "high-powered assault rifles?"

Laughably, gun control proponents often cannot decide how they want to demonize these guns, and it makes for some interesting contradictions.

Following the November 2004 slayings of six deer hunters in a racially charged incident in northern Wisconsin by an immigrant from Southeast Asia who was armed with an SKS-type rifle, the Brady Campaign to Prevent Gun Violence declared that such rifles are not suitable for deer hunting because they fire "underpowered" cartridges. However, in a seething editorial published by *The Capital Times* in Madison, the newspaper blasted the use of SKS rifles for deer hunting, calling this gun "a high-powered semiautomatic...carbine."

Well, which is it? Both descriptions cannot be correct.

The newspaper also inserted its journalistic foot further in mouth by declaring "Semiautomatic weapons are increasingly popular among hunters of a not particularly sporting ilk." That was before Sawyer County, WI Sheriff James Meier told the Eau Clair *Leader-Telegram* that some of his deer hunting partners used SKS rifles in the Wisconsin deer woods. Indeed, semiautomatic rifles manufactured by Winchester, Remington and Browning that used more powerful ammunition had been in use by Wisconsin deer hunters for generations, and prior to the Vang killings, nobody at *The Capital Times* had raised so much as an eyebrow about that.

In 2004, prior to the expiration of the ten-year "ban" on so-called "assault weapons," author Workman revealed in a widely-published opinion column that newspapers could not even get their stories straight about the frequency in which such guns are used in crimes.

An April 30, 2004 editorial in the South Bend, Indiana *Tribune* stated, "In 1993, prior to the ban, assault weapons accounted for 8.2 percent of all guns used in crime. After the ban had been in effect for three years, the proportion had dropped to 3.2 percent."

Contrarily, two days later, the *New York Daily News* editorialized, "Before the federal ban, assault weapons were used in almost 5% of crimes. After the ban, that number dropped to 1.6%."

According to veteran researcher David Kopel with the Independence Institute, a Colorado-based think tank, in 1990 in California – four years before the ban was instituted – only 58 of the 1,979 guns seized from drug dealers were classified as "assault weapons." Between 1985 and 1989 in Chicago, only one murder was committed with a rifle firing a military-caliber cartridge, and in 1989 Chicago police seized 17,144 guns, only 175 of which were "military-style weapons." Also in 1989, New Jersey authorities reported not a single homicide involving a rifle of any kind.

"Incidentally," Workman wrote, "in Chicago, according to FBI data, the chance of being stabbed or beaten to death is 67 times greater than being murdered with a so-called 'assault rifle'."

"Between Jan. 1, 1989 and Dec. 31, 1993 – again prior to the ban – Miami, Fla. police seized 18,702 firearms, of which only 3.13 percent were considered "assault weapons," according to Kopel. Nationally, he noted, less than four percent of all homicides involve any kind of rifle, and no more than 0.8 percent of these guns fire a "military caliber" cartridge.

How odd, then, that during his acceptance speech for the Democratic nomination in the summer of 2008, Sen. Obama would cling to the now-discounted notion that the AK-style rifle is commonly used by criminals, when it has been proven statistically that this is not the case.

Said Obama: "The reality of gun ownership may be different for hunters in rural Ohio than for those plagued by gang-violence in

Cleveland, but don't tell me we can't uphold the Second Amendment while keeping AK-47s out of the hands of criminals."

What troubles gun rights advocates with such statements is that gun prohibitionists envision only one strategy available to keeping any firearms out of criminal hands, and that is a total ban on the private ownership of firearms. That the Supreme Court in June 2008 ruled the Second Amendment to be protective of an individual civil right to keep and bear arms seems only a small inconvenience to the prohibitionist, who now approaches the "gun problem" as being one of strict regulation. Ultimately, they will argue that gun ownership should be regulated to the point that most citizens are discouraged from having firearms because the regulations would be too onerous.

In the seemingly endless debates over adoption of concealed carry laws in dozens of states that have enabled increasing numbers of law-abiding private citizens to be armed in public as a preventive or proactive measure against criminal attack, the press quickly adopted a term "hidden handgun" that was a product of the anti-gun lobby. Opponents of concealed carry, as noted earlier, have testified before virtually every state legislature considering reform statutes with dire predictions of increased violence, more body counts, and the dangers that "hidden handguns" pose to children (though never explaining just what those dangers are), typically without being challenged by the press corps on any of these allegations.

The rhetoric in each one of these efforts seems canned as though it had been taken from the same page of a gun control playbook.

The term "hidden handgun" deliberately relays the impression that the armed citizen is up to no good. In the 19th Century that actually was the common philosophy because most armed citizens openly carried their guns, and nobody considered that unusual. If a person did not have a pistol, then perhaps a dagger, cane sword or some other defensive weapon was carried. It was considered the lot of a scoundrel to conceal a pistol. Perpetuating that impression today is an element of the campaign to demonize guns and their owners.

The effectiveness of the campaign against concealed carry might best be demonstrated by the remarks of an individual who participated in a rather heated discussion of gun laws in the *Denver Post* on June 24, 2008. As is normal with people who habitually participate in such newspaper feeback discussions, this individual had a nickname to conceal his or her identity. But it was what this person wrote that underscores the vile nature of the opposition to legally-armed citizens:

"The last thing we need is a bunch of gun nuts staggering out of some bar drunk and deciding that they need to 'protect' themselves. It's hard enough to hit a target sober but allowing a bunch of insecure nut jobs all jacked up on liquor acting as judge jury and executioner will get some innocents killed. They all want to cry about their 'rights' to carry but what about the rights of others to be safe from the irresponible (sic) and irrational actions of drunken insecure Dirty Harry wannabes? Let the cops handle it."

During the debate over legalizing concealed carry in Wisconsin, one police official, Lisbon Police Chief Patrick Clarey, stated his opposition to that personal protection legislation by observing, "I don't want to go back to the days of the wild, wild West with people settling their disagreements in a shootout at the mall." This is yet another form of demonization; suggesting that legally-armed private citizens pose a clear danger to the public at large because they might start a gunfight over some trivial matter in a public venue.

How many times have editorial writers, anti-gun politicians and gun prohibitionists alluded to "the gun show loophole?" This so-called "loophole" is actually a provision in federal law that has allowed undocumented private sales of firearms between individuals for many years.

While the term is used by the Brady Campaign to Prevent Gun Violence to instill a belief that gun shows are "arms bazaars for criminals and/or terrorists," there is no basis in fact to characterize gun shows in this manner. A study for the Department of Justice that surveyed several thousand convicted felons revealed that less than one percent (0.7 percent) of these individuals got their guns at gun shows. We mentioned this earlier, in Chapter 5.

The Brady Campaign disputes this, pointing to a mid-2000 report from the Bureau of Alcohol, Tobacco, Firearms and Explosives called *Following the Gun: Enforcing Federal Laws Against Firearms Traffickers*. This report was issued at the end of a two-year investigation undertaken during the Clinton Administration and it asserted that 'Gun shows were a major trafficking channel, involving the second highest number of trafficked guns per investigation (more than 130), and associated with approximately 26,000 illegally diverted firearms. The investigations involved both licensed and unlicensed sellers at gun shows."

Kopel, writing for the Cato Institute in January 2000 noted that, "According to an (National Institute of Justice) study released in December 1997 ('Homicide in Eight U.S. Cities,' a report that covers much more than homicide), only 2 percent of criminal guns come from gun shows.

"That finding is consistent with a mid-1980s study for the NIJ, which investigated the gun purchase and use habits of convicted felons in 12 state prisons. The study (later published as the book *Armed and Considered Dangerous*) found that gun shows were such a minor source of criminal gun acquisition that they were not even worth reporting as a separate figure.

"At the most recent meeting of the American Society of Criminology, a study of youthful offenders in Michigan found that only 3 percent of the youths in the study had acquired their last handgun from a gun show. (Of course some criminal gun acquisition at gun shows is perpetrated by "straw purchasers" who are legal gun buyers acting as surrogates for the individual who wants the gun. Straw purchases have been federal felonies since 1968.)

"According to the educational arm of HCI (Handgun Control, Inc. the former title of the Brady Campaign), the group's own survey of major-city police chiefs found only 2 out of 48 who said that guns from gun shows (both 'legal and illegal sales' according to the questionnaire) were a major problem in their city."

A favorite term of the gun prohibitionist vocabulary is "gun nut." Trivial as it seems, this term suggests that a person who is interested in firearms may be mentally or emotionally unstable. Even Wikipedia acknowledges that the term is sometimes "regarded as a pejorative stereotype cast upon gun owners by anti-gun advocates as a means of implying that they are fanatical, exhibit abnormal behavior, or are a threat to the safety of others."

Alan Korwin, a noted author and public speaker on gun rights issues, assembled a list of terms, and their translations, that are most often employed by gun prohibitionists.

For example, "common sense gun laws" actually mean "public disarmament laws," according to Korwin. "Closing the gun show loophole" means simply closing gun shows.

While the various buzz words and catchy phrases have been effectively used to push the gun control agenda, the firearms community has increasingly taken the gun control vocabulary and turned it against the anti-gun lobby.

Among gun enthusiasts, new concealed carry legislation is both "sensible" and "responsible" or "reasonable."

The term "gun nut" is now used among gun owners as one of tongue-in-cheek affection, and even veteran outdoor writer David Petzal has a column in a nationally-circulated outdoors magazine called "The Gun Nut."

"Assault weapons" have become "sport/utility rifles."

And for firearms rights advocates, "Gun control is being able to hit your target."

Although the firearms community has adopted many of these terms in a self-deprecating manner, there remains a serious concern that there is a more sinister motive behind the gun control movement. As many gun rights advocates suggest, the concern is that the focus of prohibitionists is "gun" but the ultimate goal is "control."

They amplify their contention by pointing to an observation from one of America's great thinkers, the late Noah Webster.

"Before a standing army can rule," Webster wrote, "the people must be disarmed; as they are in almost every kingdom in Europe. The supreme power in America cannot enforce unjust laws by the sword; because the whole body of the people are armed, and constitute a force superior to any band of regular troops that can be, on any pretence, raised in the United States. A military force, at the command of Congress, can execute no laws, but such as the people perceive to be just and constitutional; for they will possess the power, and jealousy will instantly inspire the inclination, to resist the execution of a law which appears to them unjust and oppressive."

Not coincidentally, among firearms owners it is a common if not universal philosophy that individual liberty and self-reliance are the principles upon which the United States was founded and which have made it great today.

Conversely, those who had long insisted the Second Amendment only protected some right of the states to organize militias subscribe to a "collectivist view" that dismisses the individual right theory. Even in the wake of the 2008 Supreme Court ruling in the case of *District of Columbia v Heller*, these gun prohibitionists insist the high court was wrong. This philosophy is not limited to gun ownership. Gun control proponents insist that the police are able to protect people from criminals, and that individuals should refrain from taking direct action against criminal attack.

In the vernacular of gun rights individualists, this amounts to a "Nanny State" mentality under which it is perceived that the state can provide for people better than they can, themselves. Activists such as Vanderboegh maintain that the firearm provides citizens the only means to ultimately resist being co-opted by an oppressive government, which is precisely what many gun rights activists insist the Second Amendment was truly all about.

One is reminded of the fictional Borg Collective in the *Star Trek: The Next Generation* television series. The Borg was a species consisting of part machine, part living being, and their mantra consisted of a single phase: "Resistance is futile."

Not so for the free man who is armed and willing to resist. Such individuals are the targets of anti-gun demonization; stereotyped as being unreasonable and lacking the "common sense" to acquiesce to all variety of restrictive gun control measures. They become the "gun nuts" to be viewed suspiciously by their neighbors and acquaintances; individuals living on the margins of society who may be on the verge of snapping and causing some great harm to the community.

Gun prohibitionists have long alluded to the number of homicides in America as a reason to crack down on gun ownership, while never acknowledging that not all homicides are committed with firearms.

As author Workman noted in a late 2007 column published in several newspapers, "In 2002, rifles were identified as the weapon used in only 488 of the 9,528 homicides involving firearms. In 2006, the most recent year for which data is available, rifles were used in 436 of the 10,177 gun-related homicides.

"Curiously, between 2002 and 2006," he continued, "the use of knives as murder weapons actually increased, while the use of shotguns remained pretty much level, at 486 and 481 homicides, respectively.

"Since 1994, the year that Congress banned certain types of semiautomatic firearms, the incidence of murder and 'non-negligent manslaughter' has declined, even though this ban expired in 2004. In

1994, there were 23,326 murders in the United States, according to FBI data. In 2006, that figure dropped to 17,034 slayings, a figure that nobody should feel is acceptable, but demonstrates that homicides declined during a period when gun ownership increased dramatically in the United States."

Take note of two figures Workman highlighted: The total number of murders in 2006 (17,034) and the number of those killings that involved firearms (10,177). Certainly, this is not a good statistic, but it does refute the illusion created by gun control lobbyists that all American homicides are gun-related.

Gun prohibitionists frequently assert in letters to local newspapers that "guns kill 30,000 people a year in this country." This would only be accurate if one includes all of the suicides and accidents. However, the figure is traditionally used in an effort to convince people that all of these deaths are somehow crime-related and that is simply not true. As the saying goes, "truth is the first casualty of war," and there should be no doubt that a war over private gun ownership is being waged in the United States.

In a late-2008 fund-raising appeal, Sarah Brady wrote, "As soon as President-elect Obama is inaugurated and the 111th Congress is sworn in, the Brady Campaign will be making an all-out push to advance our lifesaving legislative agenda... But that doesn't mean we are waiting until Inauguration Day."

The choice of words here, as elsewhere in statements issued by the Brady Campaign, subliminally posits that people who oppose their legislative agenda are not interested in saving lives. The Brady Campaign also contends that the inability of Congressional gun control enthusiasts to push the Brady agenda under President George Bush had turned America's streets "into shooting galleries." It was not true, but it did manage to plant the image in someone's mind that policies supporting individual gun owner rights somehow made neighborhood streets less safe. The message also telegraphs the impression that there is a problem, and the Brady Campaign is going to do something about it.

CHAPTER 8

The Campaign of Litigation

Unable to legislate lawful firearms ownership out of existence, gun control extremists have turned their fanatical attention to the courts in recent years, in a campaign designed to financially bleed and ultimately destroy the firearms industry via economic attrition.

Although the gun ban lobby had successfully pushed a Democrat-controlled Congress to pass two pieces of "trophy legislation" during the first two years of the Bill Clinton administration – the 1993 Brady Law and the 1994 ban on so-called "assault weapons" that subsequently expired in September 2004 – after Republicans were swept into office by gun owner backlash, gun control measures did not fare well on Capitol Hill.

Likewise, state legislatures began enacting "shall issue" concealed carry statutes and "preemption" laws that prohibited cities and counties from adopting their own gun laws. These developments infuriated gun banners because they enabled millions of American citizens to obtain concealed carry licenses and permits – previously issued at the discretion of local police chiefs and sheriffs as perks to political supporters and well-connected citizens – and pack defensive firearms peaceably. They also nullified the ability of anti-gun local politicians to perpetuate a checkerboard system of gun laws that were frequently in conflict with state statute or the state constitution.

Perhaps what angered gun control proponents the most was that these liberalized concealed carry statutes and state preemption laws were followed by declines in violent crime. It seemed to horrify the gun ban lobby that the presence of an armed citizenry had something of a dampening effect on criminal activity, and that the public, previously resistant – or even philosophically hostile – police officials and even the press in many cases took notice of the trend. While newspaper editorials dared not acknowledge that their opposition to concealed carry reform had been proven wrong, some newspapers published reports citing the downward trend in crime in the wake of the adoption of such statutes, and these stories sometimes included admissions by police officials and sheriffs that their original opposition had been unfounded.

So, a new attack strategy was adopted by gun ban lobbying organizations. Instead of depending upon their political allies in Congress and state legislatures to push their agenda of public disarmament, they turned to the courts, expecting liberal judges to do what lawmakers would not by essentially legislating from the bench.

While legal actions against various gunmakers were invariably touted as attempts to make them "act more responsibly," in truth these civil tort complaints sought millions of dollars in damages or compensation, and to establish a degree of liability for the criminal misuse of products previously unheard of; a level of manufacturer responsibility that, had it been applied to auto companies and liquor distillers for drunk driving fatalities, would have put both industries out of business.

There was no small amount of irony in these legal actions, because they almost universally avoided touching on the subject of "product liability" because the firearms worked as they were designed to work. Somebody pressed the trigger, and the gun fired.

This campaign of litigation began in 1989 with the founding of the Legal Action Project of the Center to Prevent Handgun Violence, later to become an arm of the Brady Campaign to Prevent Gun Violence. This organization began legal actions in an effort to establish manufacturer liability for crimes and accidents involving firearms. At its helm is Dennis Henigan, who has waged a legal battle against guns and gun makers for more than two decades.

Lawsuits were filed against gun companies for the accidental deaths of individuals, one of the more celebrated of these being the case against Beretta USA over the accidental shooting death of a 15-year-old youth in Oakland, California.

Another case was filed against a gun shop owner who had sold more than 60 handguns over a 24-month period to an alleged gun trafficker. Two of those guns were subsequently sold to a white supremacist who used them in a racially-motivated attack.

It is a war of attrition that has so far cost the firearms industry more than $250 million, and there is no indication that the gun ban lobby and the municipal officials under its control have any intention of abandoning the strategy, despite federal legislation that bans such lawsuits.

Henigan is the man who once notoriously recited the Second Amendment as "A well-regulated militia, being necessary to the security of a free state, the right to keep and bear arms shall not be infringed." He noticeably left out three significant words that defined to whom the right was endowed: "of the people." The full wording of the Second Amendment is "A well-regulated militia, being necessary to the security of a free state, the right *of the people* to keep and bear arms shall not be infringed."

This statement had appeared for some time on an Internet video clip, and is still available at the "Armed and Safe" website. His remarks were made after the District of Columbia Court of Appeals ruled in favor of the original plaintiffs in the Second Amendment Parker case, but before the Supreme Court defined the Second Amendment in the landmark ruling in *District of Columbia v. Dick Anthony Heller* (which began as *Parker v. District of Columbia*) on June 26, 2008.

It was probably no accident that Henigan omitted those three critical words from his recitation. Anti-gunners have never thought that the Second Amendment protected and affirmed an individual civil right, although only Henigan has apparently ever had the audacity to essentially edit the wording of the Second Amendment to fit his personal agenda, while on camera. That was, after all, a cornerstone of their argument against the Heller case, that the Second Amendment only protected some sort of "collective right" of the states to form militias. Even now, after the Supreme Court has defined the Amendment as it was always meant to be defined, and as the Founders understood it, the gun control lobby follows a political strategy that removes any doubt they believe the right may be literally regulated to the level of irrelevancy.

As Ted Novin, public affairs director for the National Shooting Sports Foundation (NSSF) noted in an interview for this book, the Heller ruling has perhaps inadvertently given gun control proponents a new way to spin their argument. They can now claim, he observed, that the threat to gun ownership has been removed by affirming the individual right to keep and bear arms.

"Since guns can't be banned, there's no real threat," Novin said, explaining the new rhetoric of the gun control lobby, "but the reality of it is that you can regulate firearms out of existence."

Novin has absolutely no doubt that the underlying goal of these municipal lawsuits was to bankrupt the gun industry.

"I think (that's) absolutely right," he concluded.

NSSF is an industry umbrella organization that includes some 4,700 members from all corners of the firearms and outdoors industry, including gun makers, optics companies, accessories manufacturers, retailers, distributors and even outdoor publications.

At least part of the blame for the continued push for restrictive regulations must rest with Supreme Court Justice Antonin Scalia, whose majority opinion in the Heller case noted "Like most rights, the right secured by the Second Amendment is not unlimited. From Blackstone through the 19th-century cases, commentators and courts routinely explained that the right was not a right to keep and carry any weapon whatsoever in any manner whatsoever and for whatever purpose." Among the recognized limitations, he added, would be "longstanding prohibitions on the possession of firearms by felons and the mentally ill, or laws forbidding the carrying of firearms in sensitive places such as schools and government buildings…"

Gun control advocates quickly seized on that small section of the ruling to argue that the high court had ruled that the Second Amendment is subject to "reasonable regulation" without defining the term, or what is "reasonable." To gun prohibitionists, "reasonable regulation" would include licensing, registration, limits on the type, caliber and number of firearms a citizen might own, prohibition of concealed carry, mandatory gun locks, and virtually any other restriction the anti-gun lobby conjures up, including restrictions on ammunition.

The gun ban lobby began fighting that battle anew legislatively after Barack Obama ascended to the presidency with a Democrat majority in both houses of Congress. Congressman Bobby Rush, representing the 1st Congressional District of Illinois – President Obama's home district in Chicago – introduced H.R. 45, a measure that would mandate gun owner licensing and gun registration, and passing a "competency test" that was reminiscent of "literacy tests" required of black voters in the Deep South from the late 1890s to the mid-1960s until passage of the Civil Rights Act prohibited such testing.

Gun control groups are vowing to continue their war of litigation. Perhaps they are emboldened by what to them appears to be a "bullet proof" Democrat majority, and the fact that they have an avowed anti-gunner in the Oval Office.

While the gun ban lobby spent a few years during the first part of the Clinton Administration challenging gun companies with individual lawsuits, the real campaign to bankrupt the firearms industry was built around a series of municipal lawsuits launched by liberal big city mayors and their administrations during the first months of Bill Clinton's second term.

The first legal bow shot was fired in October 1998 when then-New Orleans Mayor Marc Morial announced that the Crescent City had filed a lawsuit against ten gun manufacturers. It was the first time in history that an American city had sued the firearms industry. Over the next several months, with no small amount of encouragement from major gun control lobbying groups, other cities filed municipal lawsuits against gun makers. The list included Los Angeles, San Francisco, Boston, Cincinnati, Chicago, Miami-Dade County and Atlanta. By the time these municipal lawsuits were all filed, the firearms industry found itself under attack by more than two dozen cities.

On December 7, 1999 – ironically Pearl Harbor Day – the Clinton Administration joined in the attack, announcing that it was also preparing a legal action against the firearms industry. This would be a class-action lawsuit representing local public housing authorities that administered largely inner-city housing projects, where violent crime was rampant.

In June 2000, the City of New York – under then-Mayor Rudolph Giuliani – and several others filed a lawsuit that came to be known as *City of New York v. Beretta*. This complaint alleged that firearm manufacturers and distributors were using marketing practices that amounted to a "public nuisance." It should be noted that Giuliani's inauguration of this lawsuit was later to become one of the reasons he was not inaugurated as president of the United States in 2009. When Giuliani launched his campaign for the Republican nomination, this lawsuit and his support for other gun control measures came back to haunt him among one of the most important voting blocs upon which GOP candidates regularly depend, and all-too-often take for granted: Gun owners.

After Giuliani left office in 2002, the lawsuit was continued and zealously pursued by Mayor Michael Bloomberg.

The fundamental argument in all of these legal actions was that gun makers are responsible for the criminal misuse of their products; i.e. violent crime that left cities financially strapped on two fronts, public health care and emergency room trauma care for shooting victims, whether they were innocents or thugs deliberately shot down, and loss of property tax revenue because crime rates lowered property values in certain neighborhoods. The lawsuits contended that these losses should be recoverable by the municipal governments which had been paying for crime by having to finance health care for the victims, paying police overtime or hiring new police to combat crime, and because of the aforementioned loss of tax revenue as property values declined.

Much of the public and the courts at various levels, did not concur with the notion of industry responsibility.

NSSF's Novin observed, "Anytime you're trying to say manufacturers of a lawful product should be held accountable for the criminal misuse of (that) product…you certainly don't need to be pro-gun to consider that unjust."

As the number of lawsuits grew, NSSF established the Hunting and Shooting Sports Heritage Fund. This was a fund-raising vehicle to help fight the lawsuits and to create what Novin called "a better political environment." NSSF did the latter through education of lawmakers and their staffs, and the public.

The history of these lawsuits is detailed by author Michael I. Krauss in his booklet *Fire & Smoke*, published in 2000 by the Independent Institute.

Ratcheting up the rhetoric, mayors and those standing in the shadows feeding them their talking points also claimed that gun makers were flooding the market with more guns than could be purchased legally by legitimate consumers. The result of this saturation was that many of these guns ended up in the hands of people who should not have them, the argument went.

Ultimately, the Morial lawsuit ended up before the Louisiana Supreme Court, which dismissed the case because, by then, the Louisiana Legislature had passed a statute barring such lawsuits. The U.S. Supreme Court declined review.

A similar fate awaited the City of Atlanta's lawsuit, which was dismissed by the Georgia Court of Appeals in February 2002. By the time the lawsuit reached the appellate court, Georgia lawmakers had also passed legislation barring such lawsuits.

Ultimately, the same thing happened with the New York City lawsuit against 14 gun manufacturers in *City of New York v. Beretta*. On March 9, 2009, after years of legal wrangling – during which the Supreme Court upheld the constitutionality of a federal law barring such lawsuits – the high court declined to review the case, which had been tossed out by a federal appeals court.

A lawsuit filed by the City of Bridgeport, Connecticut ultimately was dismissed by the Connecticut Supreme Court for lack of standing.

Eventually, according to Novin, 36 states would pass legislation prohibiting the kinds of legal actions mounted against the industry.

Jack Adkins, at the time director of operations for the now-defunct American Shooting Sports Council, put it bluntly in an October 1998 interview with the *Los Angeles Times* that the lawsuits were attempting "to shift responsibility for the illegal use of our products."

Essentially the same criticism was leveled by Robert W. Tracinski, senior writer for the Ayn Rand Institute, who authored an essay called "An Unjust Assault on Guns."

"Liability law," Tracinski argued, "ought to be based on the principles of individual responsibility; the idea that an individual is liable for harm caused by his own actions. But the suit against gun manufacturers seeks to shift this responsibility to an inanimate object and to its manufacturer."

Tracinski added that, if lawsuits against gunmakers were successful, every maker of every product in America would be vulnerable.

"The overthrow of individual responsibility," he wrote, "punishes manufacturers for any negative effects involving their products."

He listed liquor companies, automakers, cutlery manufacturers and a host of others that would be subject to the same kind of attack and he criticized the legal philosophy "that diverts responsibility to anyone with 'deep pockets'."

Adkins and Tracinski would ultimately be proven correct in courtroom after courtroom as the lawsuits were either dismissed or defeated. In the case of Boston, that lawsuit was dropped in March 2002, with the city citing financial impediments; it would have just cost too much to go to court. In a press release, the city claimed that it had put forth a strong case and that the firearms industry had taken steps to address many of its concerns.

What the city didn't acknowledge was that it probably would have lost, based on the track record of the other municipal lawsuits.

Buried in the *Los Angeles Times'* story, which was published on October 30, 1998, was a little-known fact about a lawsuit in New York against gun makers. The newspaper almost too casually noted that this lawsuit was funded "with the help of a $300,000 grant from a foundation headed by financier George Soros."

Soros is the billionaire-turned-political-activist, a Jewish native of Hungary who survived World War II, migrated first to England and then to the United States. He has bankrolled Far Left groups including MoveOn.org and America Coming Together.

Many if not all of these lawsuits were assisted by the Brady Campaign's Legal Action Project, and Henigan was prominently involved. They even boasted about it in a July 11, 2000 press release, claiming to "represent over two dozen of the cities and counties that have filed suits against the industry."

At that time, Henigan vowed to continue filing lawsuits even if legislation were passed that prevented such legal actions against the gun industry. By the time several of these cases had been litigated, the industry was referring to them as "junk lawsuits," and their track record in court suggested this was an accurate description.

The protective legislation to which Henigan had earlier alluded did pass, but in the years since President George Bush signed the Protection of Lawful Commerce in Arms Act on October 26, 2005, there have been lawsuits against individual firearms retailers, initiated by anti-gun New York Mayor Michael Bloomberg.

The courtroom strategy had shifted. Instead of targeting groups of firearm manufacturers, Bloomberg went after individual gun dealers, who did not have the financial resources to battle the billionaire mayor in court. Many of them reached settlements with Bloomberg, and at least one closed her doors and went out of business.

One Georgia-based gun store, Adventure Outdoors, filed a counter-suit against Bloomberg.

In early 2006, Bloomberg and Boston Mayor Thomas Menino invited 15 mayors from around the nation to a gathering at Gracie Mansion in New York City. This "summit" came just a few weeks before Bloomberg announced that New York was filing lawsuits against 15 separate gun dealers in five different states.

The mayors' summit was the launching pad for a group calling itself Mayors Against Illegal Guns (MAIG). The problem with this coalition was that it could not, and would not define what an "illegal gun" is, because there is really no such thing outside of New York or Chicago, where guns have to be registered. In the eyes of the MAIG group, any gun in the hands of a private citizen was potentially illegal, and in one instance involving Seattle Mayor Greg Nickels, even legally-concealed handguns would eventually be targeted as being illegal on Seattle-owned city property.

A week after returning to Seattle from the Gracie Mansion "summit," Mayor Nickels announced a gun control package that targeted gun shows, using a tragic shooting in his city the previous year as his motivation. Local gun rights activists were quick to note that the firearm used by the shooter in that incident was not purchased at a gun show. Indeed, there appears to be no correlation at all between gun shows and any shooting in Seattle.

Unknown to the public, at the time Bloomberg and Menino formed their coalition of mayors, Bloomberg was preparing to launch his multi-state lawsuit. He had dispatched private investigators – not police officers – to conduct what amounted to illegal "straw man" purchases of firearms. While the press essentially gave Bloomberg a free ride on this litigation – nobody questioned why Bloomberg had filed civil lawsuits rather than turn over the results of his investigation to law enforcement agencies – gun rights organizations, the firearms industry and the NSSF quickly declared the "investigation" to be nothing more than a publicity-seeking rogue operation that quite probably violated several state and federal statutes.

In an unusual turn of events, that position was reinforced when officials at the federal Bureau of Alcohol, Tobacco, Firearms and Explosives (ATF) also criticized Bloomberg's sting. ATF had been accused by Bloomberg of being essentially asleep at the wheel for not putting the targeted gun dealers out of business.

However, it soon became evident that Bloomberg's maverick "gun sting" operation may have interfered with legitimate, on-going investigations. Instead of meekly sitting back and allowing Bloomberg to use the ATF as his personal political whipping boy, the agency launched its own investigation of the mayor's questionable operation. Sources at the ATF's Washington, D.C. headquarters told author Workman at the time that the agency was furious with Bloomberg for jeopardizing not only its investigations, but for potentially placing undercover agents at personal risk. This was more than retaliation by an agency that had become infamous for the conduct of some agents in the field during highly-dramatized raids on alleged gun law violators. This was a serious reaction with potential legal ramifications to Bloomberg's politically-motivated operation because it apparently interrupted genuine law enforcement efforts.

Five months after the Second Amendment Foundation – a Bellevue, Washington-based firearm civil rights group – called upon then-Attorney General Alberto Gonzales to investigate the Bloomberg "sting," an official with the ATF confirmed that an investigation was underway. By now, it was early 2007, and a few days after the agency revealed that an investigation had been in progress, an official with the Department of Justice advised Bloomberg's office that the mayor could face "potential legal liabilities" for the sting.

In a letter signed by Michael Battle, director of the executive office for United States Attorneys at the Justice Department, Bloomberg's office was admonished for undertaking the rogue operation. Adding insult to injury, Battle advised Bloomberg that the

Justice Department would not be filing any charges against any of the 15 gun dealers targeted by the mayor's operation.

Battle also warned Bloomberg that such undercover operations conducted by private investigators lacked "proper law enforcement authority."

Publicly, Bloomberg appeared unfazed by the stern Justice Department warning. However, he did not tempt fate by immediately launching a follow-up sting operation, instead turning his attention to Capitol Hill, where he began lobbying Congress to repeal legislation that prevents him and other municipal governments from accessing sensitive gun trace data maintained by the ATF.

Bloomberg and other mayors want to tap that information so they can use it to fuel more municipal lawsuits against gun manufacturers, despite the fact that such lawsuits are prohibited by the 2006 legislation. One might reasonably question such arrogance; filing lawsuits they know are not permitted by law, and which they may privately acknowledge have little chance of success. What else does one call such legal actions other than junk and harassment? To what other conclusion about these lawsuits could one arrive than to categorize them as an attempt to financially cripple a legal business?

There is nothing in the Protection of Lawful Commerce in Arms Act that prevents a legitimate lawsuit for producing a faulty product, or for deliberately selling a firearm to someone who does not clear a background check, for example. To argue otherwise is to engage in prevarication, and Mayor Bloomberg and his colleagues know it.

Likewise, and contrary to what Bloomberg and others have claimed, legislation that protects the sensitive gun trace data does not prevent police agencies from accessing that information as part of a legitimate on-going criminal investigation. Again, MAIG members and their attorneys, and every gun control lobbying organization in America knows this, and so do the politically-appointed police chiefs who have lobbied on behalf of the mayors who hired them, yet they all contend that current law prevents such access.

The litigation and lobbying to undo legislation is all tied together, NSSF's Novin suggested.

"Mayor Bloomberg and his coalition have a clear agenda," he said, "and they want to see the end of civilian ownership of firearms. They are still going to consider litigation a strong option. They are going to do everything they can to curtail the lawful ownership of firearms."

The insidious nature of such an effort is not lost on millions of Americans who are gun owners and see litigation as a back-door gun control scheme. If gun manufacturers are put out of business, the gun control lobby reasons, then ultimately the supply of firearms available to American citizens will dry up.

Perhaps Krauss put it best in *Fire & Smoke* when he wrote, "Proponents of recoupment suits...declare that they have been compelled to advocate them because the constitutional process has stymied their efforts to get their desired reforms adopted through more traditional channels. New York Senator Charles Schumer recently expressed the opinion that the courts should transform tort law to achieve public goals, since legislatures are deadlocked 'because of the peculiar way in which we elect people to office'. What these advocates of the evisceration of tort law mean is that legislatures and electorates have refused to agree with their ideas, that democracy therefore doesn't 'work' for them, and that they have decided to have their will enacted by an unelected judiciary.

"Imagine," Krauss observed, "a defeated President calling on the army to keep him in power on the grounds that he was only defeated 'because of the peculiar way we elect people to office'."

Of course, the biggest court case of them all was *District of Columbia v. Heller*, a case that the municipal government – not to mention the gun prohibition lobby – lost at the appeals court level, and then pursued to the Supreme Court, even against its own better judgment. It was the "case of all cases," the one that finally defined the meaning of the Second Amendment, interpreting it as in individual civil right, as referenced earlier in this chapter.

While Justice Scalia's majority opinion did leave gun rights activists wanting, it destroyed the core contention of the gun control movement, that the right to keep and bear arms was – as asserted by the Brady Campaign and others – limited only to service in a militia, and was some sort of "collective right" reserved to the state.

The gun prohibitionist argument was wrongly founded, as Justice Scalia detailed, on the 1939 case of *United States v. Miller*. In his dissenting opinion in *Heller*, Justice John Paul Stevens argued that "Hundreds of judges have relied on the view of the amendment we endorsed there," that the Second Amendment does not protect an individual right to keep and bear arms.

But Scalia, who repeatedly criticized the Stevens dissent, countered that "Miller did not hold that and cannot possibly be read to have held that."

The wails that followed release of the *Heller* opinion universally included the assertion that Justice Scalia had re-written history. To the contrary, Scalia had done his homework in a scholarly manner, reaching the only logical conclusion. The Second Amendment does affirm and protect a pre-existing civil right.

Yet the *Heller* ruling did not immediately nullify all gun control statutes, nor has it erected a roadblock to harassment lawsuits against gun manufacturers, wholesalers or retailers. It also will not prevent the filing of lawsuits against individual citizens whose firearms are stolen and subsequently used in a crime, if it can be argued convincingly in court that a criminal was able to gain access to the gun because it was carelessly stored. Likewise, in cases where a child is wounded or killed because a firearm was accessible, gun owners are also open to civil prosecution and in some cases criminal prosecution where so-called "safe storage" statutes have been enacted.

It is the continuing hope among gun prohibitionists that one day they will eventually win a case, thus opening the door to firearms regulation by the courts.

"They have an agenda," said NSSF's Novin. "If they can't achieve that goal legislatively they will try to ban guns through litigation."

Suing firearms manufacturers or individual gun dealers is not the only courtroom attack launched by the gun control lobby.

The Brady Campaign, in its effort to prevent people from carrying concealed in new venues, filed a lawsuit to prevent the Interior Department and National Park Service from enforcing new rules that allow licensed concealed carry on national parks and wildlife refuges. They were joined in the lawsuit by the Coalition of National Park Service Retirees and the National Parks Conservation Association.

The new regulations were adopted late in the Bush Administration and took effect on January 9, 2009, before Barack Obama moved into the Oval Office. Many in the gun rights movement believe that the primary reason the lawsuit was launched was not to protect park visitors, but to prevent the public at large from realizing that legally armed citizens are not a threat to peace and safety.

Critics of the rule change had made deliberately misleading arguments that the revised regulation would allow park visitors to engage in target shooting or hunting, and would also contribute to an increase in poaching. All of those arguments were false. The rule change only allowed legally-armed private citizens to carry concealed handguns "out of sight, out of mind" as it were.

Litigation, however, is a double-edged sword, as clearly demonstrated by the Supreme Court's ruling in the Heller case. In the wake of that landmark decision, gun rights organizations struck back.

Barely 30 minutes after the high court issued its opinion in the *Heller* case on June 26, 2008, attorneys representing the Second Amendment Foundation and Illinois State Rifle Association marched into a federal court in Chicago and sued that city over its handgun ban, which was engineered in a remarkably similar fashion to the ban that had just been nullified in Washington, D.C.

The following day, the National Rifle Association weighed in with its own lawsuit against Chicago and several surrounding suburban communities that had adopted their own handgun bans in the 1980s.

The NRA teamed up with SAF's sister-organization, the Citizens Committee for the Right to Keep and Bear Arms, to strike down a handgun ban in public housing in the City of San Francisco.

Following that victory, NRA and SAF teamed up a third time (they had been co-plaintiffs in the lawsuit that stopped the New Orleans gun confiscations following Hurricane Katrina in 2005, and against the San Francisco handgun ban ordinance passed in November 2005), filing a legal action to nullify an "alien licensing" requirement in Washington State. That statutory provision arbitrarily denied legal resident aliens of the right to possess firearms for hunting, recreational shooting, competition and personal protection.

When the District of Columbia adopted the most restrictive handgun licensing regulations it could muster, basing continued prohibitions of some handguns on a California statute that listed "good guns" and barred "bad guns" based on certain criteria, SAF went back to court to challenge the regulations. A lawsuit was filed on March 9, 2009, by SAF and three District residents, including one whose pistol was rejected simply because of its two-tone finish. The pistol was identical in design to other models of the same pistol from the same manufacturer.

That lawsuit forced the District to amend its regulations, doing away with arbitrary exclusions based on such criteria as color or the type of grips on a particular pistol or revolver. Citizens who had been previously denied an opportunity to register their handguns were invited to re-apply under the new guidelines.

By adopting the revised guidelines, the District essentially acknowledged that its previous reliance on a "roster" of "approved handguns" adopted by the State of California was faulty. California had been excluding some handguns, or dropping approved models from the "approved" roster, not because of safety concerns, but because manufacturers did not pay fees to have specific guns retained on that list.

Under the revised regulations, the District expanded its scope, utilizing "rosters" from Massachusetts and Maryland, in addition to the California roster, in determining which handguns would be approved for registration in the District.

The Heller ruling did, indeed, throw open the door for legal challenges to scores, perhaps hundreds of arbitrary firearm regulations like those in California, ranging from local ordinances to state and even federal statutes. One California attorney, Chuck Michel, frequently chuckled that the Heller ruling might easily be known as the "Full Employment Act for Attorneys."

It may take years for gun owners and organizations to roll back the layers of onerous, often contradictory laws that have been enacted since the New York Sullivan Act was adopted in the early 1900s to restrict gun possession.

CHAPTER 9

The Myth of 'Reasonable Regulation'

When gun control proponents talk about "reasonable regulations" and "sensible" or "common-sense" gun laws, the alarming truth is that they are discussing restrictions on the ownership of firearms that – were they required for the exercise of any other civil right – would be immediately challenged in court.

The gun prohibition lobby has never encountered a restrictive gun control measure that it did not deem "reasonable." Whether a scheme called for licensing of gun owners, registration (for a fee, naturally) of all firearms, mandatory training as a requirement of gun ownership or at least owning a handgun, invasive criminal and mental health background checks for the purchase of a firearm, limits on the number and types of firearms a person could own, limits on the number of firearms a person could purchase in a single month, mandatory storage regulations, ad infinitum; invariably gun control advocates considered the measure "sensible."

Take for example what the activists at Chicago's Saint Sabina Catholic Church think are "common sense" gun laws. Indeed, they think these proposals are so sensible that they put together a petition to the Illinois Legislature with the notation, "We, the citizens of Illinois, demand an end to violence in our communities! We want to stop the flow of unregulated guns and are petitioning for legislation to achieve this goal. We will push for state legislators to pass laws in 2009 that demonstrate their value for our children."

Their "common sense" proposals:

- Limit firearm purchases to one gun per month.
- Reinstate the ban on so-called "assault weapons."
- Require universal background checks (presumably on all sales at gun shows and even all private transfers, even between family members).
- Mandatory gun registration "just as we register cars."

Saint Sabina is the parish of Father Michael Pfleger, the radical priest discussed earlier

Credit is due to Pfleger and his congregation, however, for at least defining what they believe are "common sense" gun laws. Frequently, proponents of "reasonable" or "sensible" statutes are less forthcoming about what they envision as reasonable gun control. When they do, their measures may not stand constitutional scrutiny.

The Brady Campaign to Prevent Gun Violence contended that the District of Columbia handgun ban – declared unconstitutional by the U.S. Supreme Court – was "reasonable." To the contrary, the high court noted in its landmark *Heller* ruling, "The handgun ban amounts to a prohibition of an entire class of 'arms' that is overwhelmingly chosen by American society" for the purpose of personal protection. Such a ban, the court said, fails "constitutional muster."

That said, the Brady Campaign further argues that it would be "common sense" to revive and make permanent the ban on so-called "assault weapons" which are actually semiautomatic look-alikes of fully automatic military firearms, but are functionally different and are owned by millions of law-abiding American citizens. These guns are used for competition, predator control, varmint hunting and control, pest control, home protection, recreational shooting, and other legitimate purposes.

Among the people who use such firearms, they are called "sport-utility rifles," because they are, as noted above, adaptable to both sport shooting and utilitarian purposes.

None of that matters to gun prohibitionists, however. The "assault weapons" ban passed during the first Clinton administration in 1994 – a piece of legislation that ultimately cost more than 50 House

Democrats their congressional seats in the November 1994 election and shifted control of Congress to Republicans for the next dozen years – was a piece of trophy legislation for the gun ban lobby. They wailed when it was allowed to expire in 2004, and they desperately want it back on the books, forever.

Nor does it apparently matter to gun prohibitionists that a legal challenge to such an outright ban on an "entire class of arms" would almost certainly be mounted, based on the language found in *Heller*.

It evidently also does not matter that the Centers for Disease Control and Prevention released a report in 2003, more than a year before the ban expired, revealed that gun laws, including mandatory waiting periods and gun bans, had no discernible impact on violent crime involving firearms. The CDC had done a survey of gun control laws across the nation, involving a review of 51 previously-published studies about the effectiveness of gun control laws. Those studies covered virtually "all of the bases" of gun control laws, including background checks, waiting periods, bans on guns or certain types of ammunition, registration, and laws barring convicted felons from owning or buying guns.

The Brady Campaign joined with other gun prohibition lobbying groups in March 2009 following a mass shooting in southern Alabama. The perpetrator of that crime, Michael McLendon, had once tried to join a small police department, but did not complete training. On March 10, he fatally shot ten people, many of them family members including his mother, grandmother, an uncle and two cousins. He used two semiautomatic rifles in the attack.

Within hours, the anti-gun coalition led by the Brady group issued a statement calling for "an effective federal assault weapons ban to stop the mass production and marketing by the gun industry of these anti-personnel weapons. Today we call on the U.S. Congress to pass a federal assault weapons ban modeled on California's effective law that would ban these weapons once and for all."

The California statute, of course, is widely known to have been unable to disarm a single gang, nor stop a single crime. The 2003 CDC study is an "inconvenient truth" for proponents of gun bans.

At the time, according to an October 2, 2003 Associated Press story that detailed the CDC's findings, the Brady Campaign essentially dismissed the report, claiming that the laws work, but "it is nearly impossible to prove it."

The Associated Press quoted Brady Campaign spokesman Peter Hamm, who offered the incredulous observation that "It's hard to study whether gun control laws work in this country because we have so few of them."

Perhaps Hamm was unaware at the time that there are thousands of gun laws on the books, ranging from federal statutes and regulations down to local ordinances. There are myriad state laws that cover everything from concealed carry to specific regulations dealing with the type of firearms that may be used for hunting. The National Rifle Association has estimated there are some 20,000 gun laws in this country, hardly the "few" about which Hamm complained.

Hamm's remark, of course, underscores the essential philosophical problem with the gun control lobby. No matter how many laws are on the books, there will never be enough, and no matter how many new statutes are passed, it is always the *next* proposal that must be enacted.

Perhaps Hamm and his colleagues should pay attention to Lenny Mirra, a single father who wrote an opinion piece in the *Daily News* of Newburyport, Massachusetts on November 27, 2007.

"Gunphobes," he wrote, "...still have visions of sending government officials to every household in America to confiscate our guns. But that's never going to happen and a ban, in a country where there are probably more guns than people, would work only if the criminals would cooperate. They're not known for doing that."

Mirra also observed how "startling" it is that "the same exact people, who include infinite 'rights' as being protected under the First Amendment, act as if the Second Amendment doesn't exist, as if the right to keep and bear arms doesn't really mean the right to keep and bear arms."

The Brady Campaign annually grades states on their gun laws. It has become something of a ritual for a spokesman for that lobbying organization to declare that gun laws – or the lack of gun laws, actually – in most states are "abysmal."

"Most people don't realize how few laws we have on the books restricting easy access to guns," lamented Brady Campaign President

Paul Helmke in early 2009 when he criticized the State of Louisiana for its limited infringements on the right to keep and bear arms.

And what is this "easy access" to guns that Helmke and other gun prohibitionists allege?

To purchase a firearm at retail gun shops, the prospective buyer must submit to and pass a federal background check. In some states, there is a mandatory waiting period, especially for the purchase of a handgun. This waiting period may be several days in length.

Before going farther, it should be noted that these same requirements apply whether the retailer is doing business at his shop, or at a gun show. Federally-licensed gun dealers (there is no such thing as an "unlicensed dealer") cannot legally sell a firearm at a gun show without complying with all federal and state laws applying to such sales. The so-called "unlicensed dealer" is a private citizen engaged in selling a firearm in a private transaction with another private citizen, and such sales are allowed under federal law.

In California, all firearm sales must involve a background check, and that includes private party sales. This is a state statute, but the gun prohibition lobby would like this to be required in all states, for all transactions, even between family members.

In Illinois, every gun owner must have a Firearm Owner's Identification (FOID) card. In New York State, gun owners must be licensed. In New York City, license applications can be held up for six months, for no specific reason.

Another example of what gun control lobbyists consider a "sensible" firearms law is the proposal by Illinois 1st District Congressman Bobby Rush. His proposal is commonly known as the "Blair Holt Firearms Licensing and Record of Sale Act" and it is very restrictive. It would require the licensing of all handgun owners and anyone who owns any semiautomatic handgun, rifle or shotgun that accepts a detachable magazine.

The bill would also set up a federal registration system for all transfers of these so-called "qualifying firearms." Perhaps the most ominous part of the bill is that it defines "qualifying firearm" as "any handgun; or any semiautomatic firearm that can accept any detachable ammunition feeding device; and does not include any antique."

Named in memory of a heroic Chicago high school student who shielded the body of another student on a bus when a gunman boarded and opened fire, the bill would require private citizens to apply for a firearm license to the Attorney General. Prospective gun owners would be required to pass a test on safe handling and storage of firearms, the use of firearms in the home and risks associated with such use, and the legal responsibilities of firearms owners including knowledge of federal, state and local laws. Each citizen applying for a gun license would have to open his mental health records to the Attorney General "or an authorized representative" and also submit a current passport-sized photograph with their name, address and the date and place of their birth.

This license would carry a number "unique to each licensed individual," and be renewable every five years. This license can be revoked.

It would require owners of "qualifying firearms" to report any change of address within 60 days of the move, and it would also be a violation of law to not report loss of a firearm to the Attorney General within 72 hours after the loss or theft is discovered.

There is also a section relating to child safety, and it also provides for heavy fines and imprisonment for violations of the act.

Under the Rush bill, it would be illegal to sell, deliver or transfer a firearm to anyone who is not licensed. In addition, nine months after the date of enactment, this legislation requires the Attorney General to establish and maintain a federal record of sale system that would log every firearm transfer conducted in the United States that is processed by a federally licensed firearms dealer.

It also eliminates the prohibition on gun registration that is now a part of federal law.

There is an exception for "the infrequent transfer of a firearm by gift, bequest, intestate succession or other means by an individual to a parent, child, grandparent, or grandchild of the individual, or to any loan of a firearm for any lawful purpose for not more than 30 days between persons who are personally known to each other."

Under Rush's legislation, the Attorney General would create regulations that specify procedures for submission of gun license applications. These applications would be made through licensed dealers or federal agencies.

The license fee "shall not exceed $25."

Early in the Obama administration, the Brady Campaign sent a package of gun control proposals to the Obama administration that called for "a law that treats handguns like cars, with handgun owners required to be trained in safe storage and handling of guns; and with sales recorded to help stop interstate gun trafficking." This package was a 16-page document titled *Gun Violence in America: Proposals for the Obama Administration.*

Essentially, these proposals would establish *de facto* registration of handgun owners and their handguns.

The Brady Campaign's "wish list" also called for restriction of semiautomatic rifles and so-called ".50-caliber sniper rifles," to the police and military, thus banning them from ownership by private citizens. A ban on certain semiautomatic firearms and full-capacity magazines enacted under the Clinton administration in 1994 expired in September 2004. There has not been much interest in Congress except among some anti-gunners and the gun prohibition lobby to revive that ban. When it was suggested by Obama Chief of Staff Rahm Emanuel, House Speaker Nancy Pelosi was quick to counter that Congress is not interested in reviving the ban.

Also among the proposals was the repeal of the Protection of Lawful Commerce in Arms Act (PLCAA), a statute that outlawed frivolous lawsuits against gun manufacturers and retailers. A spate of such lawsuits was launched in 1999 by mayors in several cities, with support from the Brady Campaign, as detailed in the previous chapter.

The Brady Campaign also wanted to restore full access to sensitive gun trace data maintained by the Bureau of Alcohol, Tobacco, Firearms and Explosives (ATF) so that anti-gun mayors could once again use that data to launch additional lawsuits against gun makers, even though such lawsuits are prohibited. This would be accomplished by repealing the Tiahrt Amendment that protects such data.

The anti-gun lobby also wanted Congress to require background checks on all firearms transactions, even between family members. They wanted the Justice Department to retain background check records on approved gun sales for 90 days. Under current law, such information is destroyed after 24 hours. Handgun owners would be required to record all sales of their personal handguns to other persons, and to undergo training in safe storage and handling. As a result, every handgun owner in the country would maintain a personal registry of their handguns, whether they were kept or sold to another individual, or given to another family member or friend.

Additionally, the Brady Campaign wanted to allow the ATF to require firearms dealers to perform annual inventory audits as a means of preventing guns from being lost or stolen.

In summation, the Brady group was urging the Obama administration and Congress to micro-manage the firearms industry at the same time Congress would essentially open the doors once again to legal actions that would drive manufacturers out of business. That is not reasonable regulation.

Claiming that "America is the sole high-income, industrialized country that has not responsibly addressed the problem of gun violence," the Brady Campaign incredulously insisted that every one of its proposals "(is) clearly constitutional under the US Supreme Court's recent Second Amendment decision in *District of Columbia v. Heller.*"

Capping their list of "reasonable" regulatory suggestions, the Brady Campaign urged Congress to enact legislation that subjects firearms to the same consumer product safety regulation that covers virtually all other consumer products. There would be no allowance for the rigorous standards already established by the Sporting Arms and Ammunition Manufacturers Institute (SAAMI).

Perhaps the most outrageous proposal deemed "reasonable" was the one put forth by the *Chicago Tribune* in an editorial dated June 27, 2008, the day after the Supreme Court ruling in the *Heller* case. The newspaper argued that the Second Amendment should be repealed.

In what can only be defined as a monumental case of denial, the *Tribune* insisted that the Second Amendment "was intended to protect the authority of the states to organize militias."

Adding further insult to the intelligence of anyone who had followed the *Heller* case, read the ruling and understood the issue in its entirety, the *Tribune* asserted, "We can argue about the effectiveness of municipal handgun bans such as those in Washington and Chicago. They have, at best, had limited impact. People don't have to go far beyond the city borders to buy a weapon that's prohibited within the city.

"But neither are those laws overly restrictive," the newspaper continued. "Citizens have had the right to protect themselves in their homes with other weapons, such as shotguns."

The author of this editorial conveniently overlooked the fact that *all* firearms in Washington, D.C. under the law that had just been declared unconstitutional, had to be rendered inoperable. That means that even if someone had a shotgun in their home, in the event of a life-threatening confrontation, that shotgun the newspaper recommended for home defense would still be disabled, and incapable of immediate self-defense use.

Yet the newspaper considered such a law to be not "overly restrictive."

In the wake of the *Heller* ruling that declared the District's handgun ban unconstitutional, the city adopted standards that included a requirement that all handguns be "approved," and that resulted in a roster of handguns that would be allowed. Guns not on the approved roster were not allowed, even if they were different colored-models of pistols that were allowed.

And that is where Tracey Ambeau Hanson, an African-American resident of the District, steps in. Ms. Hanson's pistol of choice was a .45-caliber Springfield Armory XD-45. Now, the make and model of that pistol was on the District's approved roster, but unfortunately, not the version she picked, which had a two-tone finish. Guns on the approved roster had to be a single solid finish, blue or OD green, for example.

Ridiculous? That was the conclusion at which the Second Amendment Foundation arrived in March 2009 when it filed a federal lawsuit against the District and Police Chief Cathy Lanier over the arbitrary regulations. SAF and Hanson were joined in the legal action by the husband and wife team of Paul and Gillian St. Lawrence. They were represented in court by attorney Alan Gura, the man who successfully argued the Heller case before the U.S. Supreme Court.

Author Gottlieb, in an opinion piece circulated to every newspaper in the country was brutal on the city's attitude.

"Instead of complying with the court ruling," Gottlieb wrote at the time, "and allowing city residents to have operable handguns, rifles and shotguns in their homes, the city has thrown up one roadblock after another in its attempts to discourage the citizens it serves from exercising their constitutionally-protected individual civil right.

Naturally, opponents of private gun ownership do not see it that way. In their view, obtaining a firearm should be a very difficult process. Anti-gunners want difficulty built into the process in order to discourage as many citizens as possible from going through all of the bureaucratic hoops merely to exercise a fundamental civil right."

Essentially, despite the Supreme Court's ruling that the Second Amendment protects a fundamental individual civil right, the gun prohibition lobby continues to treat this right as though it were a privilege. As a privilege, owning a gun would be subject to all forms of regulation.

The product of such regulation, in the ideal world of the gun prohibitionist, would be a crime-free environment. That has not been the case, as noted earlier in this chapter with the result of the CDC study on the effectiveness of gun laws. There simply is not credible evidence that any gun law has resulted in a reduction in crime, regardless what proponents of strict gun regulations otherwise argue.

That is the myth of "reasonable regulation." The hoped-for results never materialize, much the same as dire predictions of mass blood-letting never come true when a measure such as licensed concealed carry is adopted.

One supposes that this could be considered a tragedy, but the greater tragedy is that people who dislike firearms – the hoplophobes discussed in Chapter One – do not merely fail to understand, they refuse to understand. Where one could forgive an honest ignorance of fact, it is not forgivable for individuals or organizations to deliberately ignore or willfully dismiss evidence simply because to accept it would lead to a conclusion they find loathsome. To do so would require an acknowledgment that everything they believe is wrong.

CHAPTER 10

Regaining Lost Gun Rights

Tuesday, November 8, 1994 was pretty much like any other mid-Autumn day in the United States, with the exception that this was the day of the mid-term elections for the first Clinton administration term in office.

It is said by political analysts and pundits that the party in power can anticipate losing a few seats in Congress at the mid-terms, and that this election is something of a bellwether in terms of judging how a president's administration is faring with the voters.

During his first two years in office, Bill Clinton had pushed universal health care with his wife, Hillary Rodham Clinton, leading that charge. It was rejected.

He had passed the Brady Gun Control Act of 1993 – parts of which were later found to be unconstitutional by the U.S. Supreme Court – and earlier in 1994, he pressured Democrats in Congress to pass a crime bill that included a ten-year ban on so-called "assault weapons." Clinton did not have the votes, or the political capital, to make the ban permanent, though he clearly wished to do so. But the ten-year "trial run" on the ban was the result of a hard-fought compromise between Congressional anti-gunners and the gun prohibition lobby, and gun rights organizations and activists.

The ban had taken effect in September, and somewhere below the radar of network news anchors and political commentators, an army of gun owners – a voting bloc that sometimes didn't vote and

The President Clinton Debacle

frequently seemed more content to fight amongst themselves – was boiling with rage. This massive army of angry gun owners-turned-activists were about to make political history, administering an object lesson in the process that still haunts the Democratic Party today.

By the time dawn broke over the United States on Wednesday, November 9, more than 50 Democrats who had voted for the gun ban and the Brady Law – ignoring their gun-owning constituents back home and instead marching in partisan lockstep with the Clinton White House – had been thrown out of office. Significant among the casualties was House Speaker Tom Foley, a Democrat representing the very conservative far eastern Washington district centered around Spokane. The 5th District is expansive, taking in Washington's famous Palouse country of rolling hills and wheat fields, the magnificent Blue Mountains and Snake River country to the south, and the rugged Selkirk Mountains and timber country to the north.

Foley, who occasionally appeared in photographs following goose hunting treks to the Columbia Basin with the late Bill Farden, founder and publisher of *Fishing & Hunting News*, had once told his constituents at a gathering in rural Newport that "They're not going to take our guns!" But Foley had allowed votes beyond the time limit, and he had also voted for the anti-gun legislation.

The 15-term congressman had other significant troubles. He had filed a lawsuit to overturn the state's term limits law, a move that infuriated voters in his district, as they had strongly supported the law. At a time when the citizens were looking rather dimly at the notion of lifetime career politicians, Tom Foley had committed an unforgiveable sin by challenging a popular law and convincing the court to strike it down. So, when the election finally arrived, voters in his conservative, pro-gun district were on the warpath.

It had been more than a century since a sitting House Speaker had been defeated in an election. This was a politically ground-shaking event, stunning the Democrat caucus on Capitol Hill, and leaving the White House agenda in a shambles. Democrats would never again control either the House or Senate while Bill Clinton remained in office.

Months later, in remarks to the *Columbus Dispatch* in Ohio, he blamed the NRA for literally changing the face of Congress, and he repeated that observation in his memoirs.

NRA had targeted Foley and dozens of other Democrats in vulnerable districts, and had hit the bull's eye. "Gun control" became a four-letter word among Democrat strategists, and for the next 12 years, many Democrats would campaign as "Second Amendment supporters" and look for every photo opportunity they could create, showing them with a gun in their hand, or at a shooting range, or in a hunting scenario. While that did not apply across the board – still several Democrats remain diehard anti-gunners – a new generation of moderate and even conservative Democrats began arriving in Washington, D.C. in 2006, and in March 2008, 65 pro-gun Democrats signed a letter to Attorney General Eric Holder, telling him that they would not support any administration effort to renew the semi-auto ban.

The 1994 Republican Revolution certainly had more "momentum issues" than simply gun control, but that one cause energized and mobilized the "gun vote" as a single issue juggernaut.

Thus began a slow, and not always successful, "march back" from years of gun control efforts that had eroded the gun rights of American citizens in many states. The 1990s would see a surge of concealed carry statutes adopted and strengthened in more than two dozen states.

Many of these statutes were either "omnibus" type bills that also changed state law to do away with local control, and put all authority for firearms regulation in the hands of state legislatures. This resulted in uniformity of gun laws within a state's borders. One city could no longer have a different set of gun ordinances than a neighboring city or a community halfway across the state.

Anti-gun mayors and city councils may have abhorred such statutory changes, and in a few cases tried to do something about it. But state lawmakers, sometimes even from the same political parties as the mayors, were extremely reluctant to surrender even part of the authority they had to the whims of municipal governments. They were not about to risk losing control of the Legislature simply to satisfy the frequently self-serving goals of a mayor.

One notable example of this political dilemma was the case in Seattle discussed earlier. Mayor Greg Nickels vowed to go to the state legislature and ask for a change in that law to allow Seattle to set its own gun laws.

But the Legislature, despite it being controlled by members of Nickels' own political party, would have none of it. Indeed, according to some political insiders, the Far Left mayor had so poisoned the political well with his promises to defy state law that he was somewhat *persona non grata* in the state capitol in Olympia. The "gun fight" was a battle that the state Democratic Caucus did not want to wage.

Washington House Speaker Frank Chopp, a Democrat and by some accounts, no friend of gun owners, was savvy enough to understand that the gun issue in the Evergreen State is political battery acid. He is also smart enough to not throw kerosene on a fire of growing public dismay over a soaring budget deficit that happened while his party has had a stranglehold on the Legislature for several years and on the governor's office for more than two decades.

In the 2008 campaign, incumbent Gov. Christine Gregoire insisted that the state's budget was balanced. Quickly after she won the election, it was revealed that the state was facing first a $3 billion deficit that soon rose to $6 billion and finally hit a plateau of $8.6 billion. House Democrats had to deal with that, and it made no sense to throw a volatile gun control issue into the mix, especially to mollify the far Left Seattle mayor.

While the situation in Washington state is but one example, gun rights activists must remember that with any effort to regain lost political ground, there must be expected setbacks. Many in the gun rights movement had become impatient, and expected (if not outright *demanded*), for example, a ruling from the Supreme Court in *District of Columbia v. Dick Anthony Heller* that would declare, once and for all time, that the Second Amendment is inviolate, that it is an absolute right, subject to no limitations.

Constitutional scholars and legal experts would balk at such a notion, observing accurately that no right is absolute and has never been held so. It is not, for example, a constitutional right to practice a religion that demands human sacrifice. One cannot use free speech or the press to slander or libel another person. One cannot organize a public gathering in order to incite a riot.

Political strategists would just as quickly explain that 69 years of legal erosion of the individual right to keep and bear arms that began with the deliberate misinterpretation and misrepresentation of the 1939 ruling in *U.S. v. Miller* would take more than a single high court ruling to reverse.

As disappointing and frustrating as it must be to Second Amendment absolutists, restoration of gun rights takes as long, if not longer, than their piecemeal erosion.

The NRA has been active and successful at the state legislative level, taking the fight to the grassroots. Tomorrow's activist is today's gun owner whose personal ox has not yet been gored by some measure.

On a different level, concentrating almost entirely on grassroots political activism and energy, the Citizens Committee for the Right to Keep and Bear Arms, and the smaller Gun Owners of America, have spurred their followers to political activism. CCRKBA has historically worked with local and state-level organizations, offering support while allowing those groups to make their own decisions. GOA has relied heavily on the Internet and various gun rights forums and chat groups to fire up its constituency.

Meanwhile, the Second Amendment Foundation (SAF) is an organization that devotes its energies to education and litigation. Over the years, it has been very successful at the latter, having filed the first lawsuit against a gun ban in San Francisco back in the early 1980s when Dianne Feinstein was mayor, and joining with the NRA in 2005 to overturn a more recent gun ban. More about legal action is reported later in this chapter.

On the political front, the gun rights issue has also gained back some lost ground among Democrat politicians. Long considered the "party of gun control," the Democrats in 2006 and again in 2008 recruited and managed to get elected several freshman Democrats to Congress who were avowed pro-gunners.

Regaining lost rights must involve different strategies.

First, on the political level, it is incumbent on the firearms community to recruit pro-gun politicians in all major parties, and work hard to get them elected, even on the local level. This is important if you are represented by someone who consistently votes against your firearm rights by supporting legislation that whittles away at those rights.

If one cannot find a pro-gun candidate, the next best strategy is to approach a candidate and educate that person on firearms rights. It is not enough for a candidate to claim "support" of the Second

Amendment. The candidate must understand why gun rights are as important today as they were at the time of the Founders. Do not be overbearing, be informative.

Grassroots political activism can take many forms beyond simply finding or educating candidates. Financial help is always necessary and welcomed by any serious candidate, especially a pro-gun challenger who is taking on a well-established incumbent.

Volunteer labor, from manning telephones at a campaign headquarters, to placing yard signs, ringing doorbells or organizing events is also important. It can pay off in the future if the challenger is elected, because gun owners will be seen as part of a community that helped secure victory.

Can't find anyone to run? Perhaps you should become a candidate! Study the issues – after all, gun owners are also taxpayers, parents, employees or employers, retired persons and/or minorities and all have more than a single issue that can appeal to voters – and run for office.

Do not forget to vote! Far too many people in the gun rights movement decline to vote, insisting that they do not believe in the system, or more self-defeating, if not self-delusional, that they "don't want their names on a list." That is nonsense.

On the activism level, join a gun rights organization, or more than one. Start with a local gun club and work up from there. The NRA, SAF, Citizens Committee for the Right to Keep and Bear Arms, Gun Owners of America; all need support from gun owners and they really are not getting it when one considers the numbers. There are an estimated 85 million gun owners in the United States, but only about 4 million NRA members, another 650,000 CCRKBA members and supporters, 600,000 SAF members and supporters, and fewer members of GOA and other gun groups. There is considerable membership overlap in those numbers.

They are carrying the political water for tens of millions of other gun owners who are perhaps acting under the illusion that gun prohibitionists are not after the firearms in *their* collections.

Important in the battle to regain lost rights is the importance of being able to conduct one's efforts in a sensible, rational manner so as not to alienate potential allies.

Do not make the mistake of thinking that the gun prohibitionists are not after *your* gun rights. It may appear that way, but it is incumbent upon firearms owners to look over the horizon. Ask yourself some questions.

What happens after "they" ban semiautomatic "assault weapons?" What class of firearms will they next go after with a campaign of demonization?

Will it be bolt-action "sniper rifles?" Included in this class of firearms would be any centerfire rifle that could be used for hunting. If it has a telescopic sight, perhaps even a black or camouflage colored synthetic stock, and worse, still, if the stock is fitted with a bipod – which is commonly used by antelope and varmint hunters, long-range competitors and others all over the country – it could easily be categorized as a "sniper rifle" by gun banners.

After hunting rifles with scopes, what would be the next logical target of gun prohibitionists? What would they go after next, perhaps semi-auto shotguns like the Browning Auto 5 used by your father and grandfather to hunt ducks and geese? Semiautomatic shotguns function essentially the same as semiautomatic rifles on the ban list. The difference is in the appearance and in the ammunition. But if a ban on one can be successfully pushed through Congress, then it is not inconceivable that a similar ban on the other would be the next step.

Certainly there would be a move to limit handgun ownership, with the ultimate intent to prohibit it altogether.

Where does one draw the line? If one is willing to acquiesce on the mere appearance of one gun over another, willing to surrender one class of firearms in hopes that such a ban will not get around to *your* firearms, willing to allow the banning or confiscation of your neighbor's guns in an effort to protect your own firearms, your cause is already lost.

To regain lost rights, one must first draw that proverbial line in the sand and take a stand. Protect your own guns by defending someone else's gun rights. Object to a ban on any kind of firearm, because the acceptance of a ban on one gun makes it that much easier for prohibitionists to come back next year or even next month with another proposed ban in a different type of firearm.

Know your state legislators, and make sure they know you. Let them know you are interested in firearms legislation, and how they vote. Ask that their office alert you to any new firearms legislation. Make sure to check with their offices at least once a month if not once a week during the legislative session.

Likewise, take the same approach with your district's congressional representative, and the two U.S. Senators representing your state. It is appalling that far too many firearms owners and self-styled gun rights activists do not know the names of their state and federal representatives.

Outside of the political arena, there are the courts.

The timing of the Supreme Court's *Heller* ruling was, according to many gun rights observers, critical to the continued defense of Second Amendment individual rights, and perhaps the first step on the "long road back" toward reclamation of lost gun rights. Had the high court ruled the other way, deciding that the Second Amendment protected only some "collective" right limited to the states, activists believe that gun prohibitionists would have pulled out all stops to outlaw private gun ownership, state constitutional provisions be damned.

The ruling allowed SAF and Illinois State Rifle Association to immediately file a lawsuit against the City of Chicago to strike down its long-standing handgun ban. That action came within minutes of the release of the Supreme Court's ruling on June 26, 2008. On the following day, the NRA filed its own lawsuit against Chicago and several surrounding suburban communities that had all banned handguns some 20 years ago, more as a symbolic gesture than as a serious crime-fighting tool.

Within weeks of the NRA's filing, the villages of Morton Grove, Oak Park, Wilmette and other nearby communities had either repealed their bans or simply were no longer enforcing them. Chicago was the holdout, and eventually, the courts combined both the SAF and NRA cases.

The legal avenue has opened up considerably since the Supreme Court ruling in the *Heller* case, but it worked significantly even before the *Heller* ruling.

A case in point occurred in the summer of 2005 following the devastation of Hurricane Katrina in and around New Orleans alluded to earlier. Authorities in the Crescent City unilaterally decided to disarm the residents, even though they acknowledged that police services had been seriously impaired.

For several days, police and National Guard units roamed the city and Lake Pontchartrain, disarming private citizens, sometimes at gunpoint. They also set up roadblocks and checked cars leaving the city, taking firearms from anyone who acknowledged there was a gun in the car.

The Second Amendment Foundation and National Rifle Association joined forces in a federal lawsuit against the city, forcing an immediate halt to the gun seizures. The city deliberately stalled, first denying any firearms had been confiscated, and then throwing up various roadblocks to return of those guns to their owners. By the time the city finally complied, many if not most of the seized guns had deteriorated so badly that they were useless.

In November 2005, only two months after joining forces in the New Orleans lawsuit, both groups were back in court together again, in San Francisco, fighting to overturn a gun ban that had been passed by public vote, in violation of the state's preemption statute.

SAF and NRA have also teamed up to overturn a long-standing statute in the state of Washington that required resident aliens to obtain a special "alien firearm license." This statute was unique to the nation – no other state had such a requirement – and when the federal government advised Washington's Department of Licensing that it would no longer conduct federal background checks for alien licensing, suddenly the state's resident alien population faced becoming "paper criminals" because they could no longer get their licenses renewed, even though they were residents in good standing, had not committed any crimes and paid taxes.

In spring 2008, the Philadelphia City Council adopted several anti-gun regulations in an effort to combat an outbreak of violence in many neighborhoods. The measures included a ban on so-called "assault weapons" and limiting handgun purchases to one per month. The NRA and National Shooting Sports Foundation quickly took action, filing a lawsuit against the city that resulted in a permanent restraining order against the ban and gun-purchase limitation.

In 2006, when a regional library system in north-central Washington State blocked adult access to Internet websites that included information on firearms and publications dealing with guns, SAF and three local residents filed a lawsuit in federal court to force the library system to allow access to the gun sites.

SAF and other gun rights organizations also have supported the long-running *Nordyke v. King* case out of California, which started as a lawsuit to overturn Alameda County's ban on gun shows, but became a mechanism to push for incorporation of the Second Amendment to the states through the Fourteenth Amendment.

Incorporation of the Second Amendment is something gun control proponents fear, as it would open the door for nullification of various gun control measures that did not pass constitutional muster under any level of scrutiny.

In the spring of 2009, SAF filed a lawsuit against anti-gun Attorney General Eric Holder, seeking federal court relief for American citizens living abroad, who were prevented by a technicality in the law from buying firearms when they visited the United States. The law requires prospective gun buyers to list their state of residence on the federal background check form. Citizens living in foreign countries have no "state of residence," so the transactions cannot go through. This is a situation that affects unknown numbers of citizens who happen to live abroad for employment or various other legitimate reasons.

SAF and two natural-born American citizens – one living in the United Kingdom and the other living in Canada – sued in federal district court in Washington, D.C. The foundation hired Virginia attorney Alan Gura, who argued the Heller case before the Supreme Court, to fight this case.

The irony of using the courts to fight back against oppressive gun laws could hardly be understated. It had taken time and the administration of George W. Bush for its appointment of conservative or moderate judges to the federal bench and the U.S. Supreme Court, to have opened this avenue for relief from gun control statutes that had, in some cases, all but emasculated the civil right to keep and bear arms. It also took serious education efforts on the part of Second Amendment scholars to bring forth evidence apparently overlooked by the judiciary and law school professors over the years. Many a law journal article dealing with the history of the Second Amendment had to be peer-reviewed, published and debated in order for judges and justices to accurately read the amendment as it was meant to be read by the authors.

It was a full reverse of the strategy that anti-gun organizations, working in concert with anti-gun municipalities, had attempted to employ in their efforts to bankrupt the American firearms industry in the late 1990s. Where lawsuits against gun makers consistently failed, however, lawsuits seeking to restore civil rights and accurately define the right to keep and bear arms as an individual right saw success, sometimes without even having to be argued in court.

As noted earlier, several communities surrounding Chicago that had adopted handgun bans in the 1980s quickly repealed those laws once they were challenged in court following the *Heller* ruling.

The process will take time and patience. Many gun rights experts candidly observe that it took more than 70 years for gun prohibitionists to pass law upon law to effectively erode firearms civil rights in the United States.

CHAPTER 11

A Looming Battle of Philosophy

Perhaps the most keen observation about the Supreme Court's ruling in *District of Columbia v. Dick Anthony Heller* in June 2008 came from California pro-gun lawyer Chuck Michel.

He called it the "Full Employment Act for Attorneys." His tongue was only part way into his cheek when he said it, because he understands what lies ahead: Years, perhaps decades of litigation challenging thousands of state and local gun regulations that have been passed over the last four generations by lawmakers who either did not believe the Second Amendment affirmed and protected an individual civil right, or that it did not apply. Arguably, some of these laws were adopted by political demagogues who simply did not care whether they were acting constitutionally.

There are many people who simply refuse to abide by the high court's majority ruling, perhaps due to years of indoctrination or because of their liberal political philosophy, and maybe they simply hate guns (or perhaps it is a combination of all three), as we discussed in the opening chapter of this book. They will continue campaigning to narrow the scope of the right to keep and bear arms until it approaches the realm of a highly-regulated privilege rather than a civil right.

Catering to these gun control holdouts are broadcast journalists and commentators, many of whom take a decidedly partisan approach to reporting or discussing firearms rights. Many in journalism have no experience with firearms; they do not own guns, they have never fired guns, they believe gun owners to be irresponsible, and they want nothing to do with hunting, shooting or any activity that involves the use of firearms.

When they adopt a more balanced approach to the topic, these journalists often find some interesting discussions with gun rights advocates.

For example, when Lesley Stahl took the CBS *60 Minutes* camera to Virginia in the spring of 2009 to discuss gun shows and firearms laws, she had a quick exchange with Philip Van Cleave, president of the Virginia Citizens' Defense League, that provided viewers with a remarkable contrast about the philosophy of gun control versus gun rights. That program aired on April 12, two days after ABC's *20/20* co-host Diane Sawyer had done a veritable hit piece on guns; a program that was so biased in its nature that it made the traditionally anti-gun *60 Minutes* program appear unusually well-balanced by comparison.

Sawyer's ABC program was called "If I Only Had A Gun." It amounted to a 60-minute infomercial against concealed carry for personal protection, and against having a firearm in the home.

After the program aired, the National Shooting Sports Foundation revealed that it had been invited "numerous times by *20/20* Senior Producer Muriel Pearson to participate." But NSSF declined, realizing that the program was "a set-up."

At the time, NSSF Public Affairs Director Ted Novin publicly reported that the organization supplied *20/20* with information on the thousands of gun laws already on the books at the federal, state and local level, along with data from the Department of Justice and the Bureau of Justice Statistics. Novin said ABC used none of that information in its 20/20 broadcast, apparently because the information "interfered with their already pre-established and desired anti-gun conclusion."

While the ABC program was decidedly biased, the CBS *60 Minutes* segment provided Van Cleave with a rare opportunity to present the gun rights position to a national audience, and to her credit as an experienced journalist, Stahl's report was quite balanced. It was candid rather than confrontational. There was one segment that offered a glimpse at the fundamental philosophical chasm that exists between the firearms community and the press, represented by Stahl, which has traditionally leaned toward the gun control side of the debate, and which arguably might be chided for failing to grasp the notion that gun owners are as sensitive about government intrusion into their affairs as are reporters over the notion of censorship.

Stahl and Van Cleave were discussing background checks on private firearm purchases between individuals, at gun shows or anywhere else. Such private transactions without background checks are perfectly legal under federal law.

Stahl: *"Why not make it uniform, have everybody go through a background check?"*

Van Cleave: *"How about making it uniform and have* **nobody** *go through the background check? The Second Amendment doesn't say 'You can get a gun if you go through a background check'."*

The exchange seemed to surprise Stahl and she did not come back with a quick retort, giving Van Cleave the final word.

It was during that segment that perennial anti-gun Senator Dianne Feinstein of California, whose first attempt at banning guns more than 20 years ago when she was mayor of San Francisco ended in a humiliating loss for her in the California courts, alarmed gun rights activists across the country. While it is true, she acknowledged, that many Democrats had been elected to Congress on pro-gun platforms and were sticking to their word, as well as their gun rights, Sen. Feinstein told Stahl that she was merely biding her time to resurrect the ban on so-called "assault weapons." She had not given up on the idea. It was, after all, a piece of trophy legislation that anti-gunners have wanted desperately to revive since it expired in September 2004.

Feinstein argued that "the National Rifle Association essentially has a stranglehold on the Congress," but Stahl noted that the White House and Congress had the nation's financial problems to fix.

Stahl: *" (President Obama has) so much on his plate right now that the idea of bringing up guns, which is considered part of the culture war, would be such a diversion."*

Feinstein: *"I agree with you. I wouldn't bring it up now."*

Stahl: *"So you're going to hold off…"*

Feinstein: *"That's correct. I'll pick the time and the place, no question about that."*

This was no secret, actually. Feinstein had earlier told reporters that she was drafting legislation to revive the ban. It is always nice to have something prepared for that "right opportunity."

Days earlier, on ABC's *Good Morning America* program airing on Monday, April 6, House Speaker Nancy Pelosi, another California liberal Democrat, acknowledged to reporter Robin Roberts that at least some members of Congress – while perhaps giving up for the time being on banning guns – would at least like to see them registered.

Gun registration has been an incendiary topic in the firearms community for many years, because historically, registration has invariably become a prelude to bans and confiscation.

Roberts: *"Under the Bush administration, you pretty much said the ball was in their court when it came to reinstating the ban. Now, it's a Democratic President, a Democratic House. So, is the ball in your court where this is concerned?"*

Pelosi: *"Yes, it is. And we are just going to have to work together to come to some resolution because the court, in the meantime, in recent months, the Supreme Court has ruled in a very- in a direction that gives more opportunity for people to have guns. We never denied that right. We don't want to take their guns away. We want them registered. We don't want them crossing state lines..."*

Feinstein and Pelosi are perhaps representative of a cadre of ranking Congressional Democrats who have learned that their kind of gun control has lost favor with the majority of American citizens, while also recognizing that those citizens change their minds with changing events. These two devoted anti-gunners, and their like-minded colleagues are merely waiting for the right tragic crime to exploit, the right catastrophe upon which to capitalize. Feinstein said so, and it is the kind of thing about which gun rights activists are concerned.

During the first months of the Obama administration, however, the gun control component of Congress could not seem to get any traction, despite a wave of violence in late March and early April that involved mass shootings in New York State and Alabama that left more than 20 people dead. Feinstein could not successfully capitalize on the slayings of four police officers by a lone gunman who used an AK-style rifle for two of those killings before he was shot fatally by responding Oakland police.

Not even the kind of public relations nightmare scenario that unfolded in Pittsburgh, Pennsylvania that left three officers dead at the hands of a young man who said he feared President Obama was going to ban guns could get Congress to take the traditionally easy course and declare war on the Second Amendment. It was, perhaps, as Lesley Stahl's *60 Minutes* report suggested: Democrats remembered what happened to their majority the last time they enacted a ban in 1994.

But this could change, and because of that, it becomes imperative that other cases reinforcing and expanding upon the *Heller* ruling be battled through the courts. This process takes years, and it costs small fortunes; money raised by advocacy groups including the National Rifle Association and Second Amendment Foundation.

The battle to roll back generations of onerous gun laws is not merely one to be waged between gun rights activists and organizations, and the governments that passed such laws. There are active and devoted gun control organizations that offer a well-funded offensive of their own to prevent such roll-backs and to promote even more restrictions.

For example, in the state of Illinois in early 2009, a petition campaign was launched in an effort to push that state's legislature to adopt what it called "Common Sense Gun Laws." Invariably, when gun prohibitionists encourage restrictive statutes, their proposals are always defined as "common sense."

Among their demands:
Limit purchases to one gun per month
Reinstate the ban on so-called "assault weapons"
Require universal background checks for any firearm transaction
Mandate that all firearms be registered, "Just as we register cars."

The last demand has been part of the gun prohibitionist "wish list" for decades, and illustrates how they view the right to keep and bear arms as a privilege. There is no right to own or drive a car. Driving is a privilege that may be revoked based on one's conduct as a driver.

Revoking someone's civil right, however, is supposed to be a thornier issue, requiring a felony conviction or a state-level misdemeanor conviction for domestic violence.

By placing a limit on the number of firearms one can purchase in a given month, it theoretically conditions the public to accept such a regulation, and prepares the public to accept a further restriction, say one gun every other month, to one gun per year, to no more gun purchases.

"Universal background checks" become a means to create a *de facto* gun registry, without having to actually push through a registration bill. It paves the way for the fourth demand, mandatory registration, by getting the public used to the idea that firearms must be registered.

The battle to prevent such a program from becoming law is waged not only in the legislatures and Congress, but in the court of public opinion, where gun owners occasionally lose ground and sometimes gain it back. The sands of public opinion are constantly shifting, though when it comes to the subject of gun ownership, since the terrorist attacks of September 11, 2001, the pendulum has been swinging farther back toward the pro-gun side of the argument, and polling data from Gallup and others show this.

Simply because this pendulum has been steadily swinging back in favor of firearms ownership does not mean that the effort to eliminate guns from society is running on empty.

However, it is not just battles with anti-gunners that are waiting over the horizon. There is a broader, and equally insidious threat, from various levels of the government, itself, that concerns many in the gun rights community.

Early in 2009, a report produced by the Missouri Information Analysis Center (MIAC) under the title *The Modern Militia Movement* surfaced on the Internet, and it set off an uproar. This report suggested that supporters of former presidential candidates Bob Barr, Ron Paul and Chuck Baldwin should be monitored because they might be connected to the militia movement.

Many gun owners supported all three candidates and Missouri is a fairly gun-friendly state. They were horrified and outraged when the report surfaced, and one Internet blogger called the report "a classic guilt by association effort designed to demonize legitimate political activity that stands in opposition to the New World Order and its newly enshrined front man, Barack Obama."

Among the things that the MIAC linked to the militia movement was the Ammunition Accountability Act, a hot button issue among gun owners.

Public outcry over this document – which was never intended for public release – resulted in the head of MIAC being transferred, and closer scrutiny on the department's activities by the Missouri Highway Patrol.

No sooner had that flap died down than a new one erupted with much broader implications. An assessment report by the

Department of Homeland Security (DHS) titled *Rightwing Extremism: Current Economic and Political Climate Fueling Resurgence in Radicalization and Recruitment* was uncovered in early April 2009. The report was issued under Obama administration's Homeland Security Secretary Janet Napolitano, the anti-gun former governor of Arizona.

Parts of the document are chilling, and reflect a fear of conservative-minded Americans by DHS that suggested an "us against them" philosophy exists within the federal agency.

"The possible passage of new restrictions on firearms and the return of military veterans facing significant challenges reintegrating into their communities could lead to the potential emergence of terrorist groups or lone wolf extremists capable of carrying out violent attacks," the report stated.

The report took every opportunity to demonize certain citizens as potential "Rightwing extremists." The term is repeated 26 times throughout the nine-page report; so much so that it might seem the agency was attempting to hammer the term into the public lexicon, or at least into the vocabulary of the law enforcement agencies and officials for whose attention the report was initially developed.

Criticism of the DHS report was immediate and blistering. Veterans' groups objected, as did conservative organizations and gun rights groups. Many believed this document reflected intolerance on the part of the Obama administration toward dissent, a notion steeped in irony, since it would put radical Leftist Obama supporters in a position of having to refute their own long-established contention that "dissent is patriotic."

"Proposed imposition of firearms restrictions and weapons bans likely would attract new members into the ranks of rightwing extremist groups," the report states, "as well as potentially spur some of them to begin planning and training for violence against the government. The high volume of purchases and stockpiling of weapons and ammunition by rightwing extremists in anticipation of restrictions and bans in some parts of the country continue to be a primary concern to law enforcement.

"Returning veterans possess combat skills and experience that are attractive to rightwing extremists," the document continues. "DHS/I&A is concerned that rightwing extremists will attempt to recruit and radicalize returning veterans in order to boost their violent capabilities."

About that same time, an interesting e-mail circulated around the country, quoting Thomas Jefferson and contrasting his words with a quote from liberal Democrat Henry Waxman, a virulently anti-gun congressman from California, in separate frames bearing their images.

In one frame, Jefferson was quoted observing: "When the Government fears the people, there is liberty. When the people fear the Government, there is tyranny."

The other frame enclosed Waxman's infamous quote, "If someone is so fearful that, that they're going to start using their weapons to protect their rights, makes me very nervous that these people have these weapons at all!"

In fairness, it must be noted that the DHS also issued a report in early 2009 that looked hard at extremist groups on the Left, specifically animal rights terrorist groups. That report was titled *Leftwing Extremists Likely to Increase Use of Cyber Attacks over the Coming Decade*. Because of the timing of its release, January 26, it is doubtless a report that was initiated by the Bush administration.

That report advised about the potential activities of groups like the Earth Liberation Front, a known domestic terrorist organization.

While this report's existence would appear to "balance the books" as it were regarding DHS intelligence activities, from another perspective it would suggest that Homeland Security is suspicious of everybody, regardless of political stripe.

There are internal battles within the gun rights community that are also looming, and these amount to more than mere sibling rivalry. As happens within any social or political movement, factions develop that occasionally threaten to fracture any organization irreparably. It should be no surprise that there are various factions within the gun rights community that do not always agree with one another, on direction or philosophy.

The firearms community is not a single-minded bloc, but a coalition of interest groups that include open carry advocates, concealed carry practitioners, competitors, hunters, owners of .50-caliber long-range rifles, black powder traditionalists, shotgun shooters and various sub-groups. Some of the individuals involved in these different factions can, at some point, be extremists while others may present themselves as moderates. In the battle for the hearts and minds of gun owners, each faction claims the high ground or the more pure philosophical position.

While leading gun rights organizations do not always get along, it would be incorrect to believe this weakens them for attack. Nothing more quickly unites these factions than a frontal assault on gun rights, and with individuals like Feinstein and Pelosi, and organizations such as the Brady Campaign or Violence Policy Center, their impatience to get everything they want – to reach for too much at one time – gets them into trouble because the threat reinvigorates firearms owners.

This was the mistake made during the first two years of the Clinton administration, passing the Brady Act in 1993 and immediately coming back with a ban on semiautomatic sport-utility rifles in 1994. While it may seem that leading Capitol Hill Democrats learned from that experience, it only seems that way, as affirmed by Feinstein's remark about finding the right time and place to rekindle the battle and fight it all over again.

In essence, the fight over gun rights versus gun prohibition will probably never end to anyone's satisfaction. Advocates on both sides come and go, and others willingly take their places, and where gun rights activists will labor to restore rights that have been eroded, gun prohibitionists will work equally hard to protect those restrictions and expand them.

The difference between the philosophies is easily summed up.

Gun owners merely wish to be left alone to live their lives as they see fit, and this largely accounts for why various factions within the firearms community do not always get along. They are individualists first and foremost. They have their own interests, and typically do not care how someone else chooses to conduct his or her affairs, so long as they do not attempt to impose their lifestyles on other individual gun owners.

Another characteristic of many 21st Century gun owners is that they are often very private about their firearms ownership, so as not to be stigmatized by the community as "one of them." Gun owners have, after all, been characterized by countless editorial cartoons, editorials and opinion pieces – as noted earlier – as less educated, perhaps paranoid, and as social misfits.

This is hardly an accurate portrayal, as firearms owners come from across the social and political spectrum. They are not easily categorized nor narrowly defined. But they are people who can take care of themselves and their families in an emergency.

Gun prohibitionists – the self-appointed gun control advocates and self-described "progressives" (a word adopted to replace "liberal" because liberals apparently dislike identifying themselves for what they arc) – may be more communal and social-dependent, envisioning a society of conformity and dependence upon one another and the overall society as a whole. Individuality tends to alarm or even frighten such people, particularly individuality associated with gun ownership, because individuality is a threat to the overall community and its conformist structure.

In simple terms, people with firearms do not need to conform, and cannot be forced to do so. They are both self-reliant and quite capable of resistance should social conditions deteriorate so drastically that resistance becomes necessary, and it is the latter capability that perhaps causes the greatest angst among the communalists who would regulate firearms strictly or ban them outright. While gun control proponents adamantly insist they are not opposed to the ownership of firearms, they are quick to add to a growing list of provisos that increasingly narrow the kinds of people for whom they believe gun ownership is acceptable while exponentially expanding the number and type of disqualifiers to gun ownership.

Essentially, from the viewpoint of the firearm owning individualist, this need for conformity is nothing less than an assault on personal liberty. Conversely, the gun prohibitionist views this ability to resist as a threat to their own freedom to expand their Utopian ideal by erecting barriers to individual conduct that fall outside of their own personal boundaries and definitions of acceptable behavior.

This "culture war" is nothing new, and the late Charlton Heston, the actor-turned-conservative activist who spent an unprecedented five years as president of the NRA, made the culture war a centerpiece of his campaign to counter the demonization of firearms and citizens who own them.

A manifestation of this cultural battle was the anti-tax/anti-big government protests organized around the nation on April 15,

2009 – tax day – by frustrated American citizens who called their demonstrations "Tea Parties" after the Boston Tea Party.

Hundreds of thousands of citizens turned out at an estimated 750 to 800 different simultaneous demonstrations around the country. While the Big Three networks, along with MSNBC and CNN, as well as local affiliates and major newspapers including the *New York Times* tried to downplay the event, under-estimate the numbers and marginalize those who attended, an accurate estimate of the turnout might go as high as 500,000 to 750,000 people. That is not a demonstration, that is a *movement*.

Certainly, among the ranks of those demonstrators were gun owners, who also happen to be taxpayers and who have been on the front lines of the fight against intrusive government for generations. What lies over the horizon could be more of the same, or a serious escalation of activity aimed at growing the size and power of government, and making it even more intrusive.

It is perhaps the final great conflict of this culture war that will be played out; the proverbial "mother of all battles" between the self-appointed "progressive" communalists and the gun-owning individualists that is almost certainly inevitable. This will be the decisive clash between two strongly divided, and divisive, cultural philosophies not only about gun ownership specifically, but in the broader sense, whether society will turn its back on individuality, or embrace it anew.

While gun prohibitionists look at every aspect of firearms ownership and gun rights, trying to find new areas to restrict or erase altogether, from attacking gun shows to banning firearms based on their appearance and ammunition capacities, the firearms community fights back.

Sincere gun rights advocates view the assault on weapons is an attack not just on firearms rights but on all civil rights. The efforts to silence gun owners politically and in more social terms, whether it be their ability to campaign for or against politicians, testify at public hearings, gather at rallies or conduct legitimate business at gun shows is viewed in the broader sense as part of a campaign to erode all liberties.

It will be up to America to see that does not happen.

CHAPTER 12

The Insidious Drumbeat for 'Tighter Gun Laws'

Throughout the history of the gun control movement – a campaign that has been shamelessly supported by a biased national press corps drifting increasingly to the Left – there has been a constant and insidious demand for "tighter" gun laws, whatever that means.

Possibly the text book example of this bias was an editorial in the Albany, New York *Times-Union* newspaper headlined "Tighten up the gun laws." Typical of such editorials, this one was leading the charge for legislation that would ostensibly prevent the kinds of shooting incidents that occurred April 3, 2009 in Binghamton, New York in which a gunman identified as Jiverly Wong gunned down 13 people at a community center before turning his pistol on himself.

New York State already has some of the "tightest" gun laws in the nation, yet Wong was able to legally purchase the handguns he carried, and had obtained a pistol permit in 1997, at which time he passed the mandated background check and jumped through all of the state's other hoops. The newspaper complained that he only had to go through the process one time, unlike motorists who must renew their driving licenses every eight years.

But the editorial writer made the same mistake about guns as many of his or her colleagues have done over the years. This editorial equated gun ownership, which is a civil right as affirmed by the U.S. Supreme Court, with driving, which is a privilege that is regulated by the state. Yet the temper of the editorial clearly shows how gun control proponents think.

Quoting the editorial, it notes that a bill, sponsored by Democrat Assemblywoman Amy Paulin and Democrat State Senator Eric Schneiderman "would require that pistol permits be renewed every five years, which already is done in New York City and Nassau, Suffolk and Westchester counties."

Calling this legislative proposal "fair and sensible," the newspaper said the bill would also require checking a gun owner's references, "typically four people who are not related to the applicant."

Further, the newspaper argued in support of the legislation that "Submitting a renewal application would automatically extend the license until the permit review process is finished, and the application is approved or denied."

Finally, the newspaper reasoned, "It's sensible, and fair, to ask gun owners to renew their licenses every few years."

How many ways can someone say "nonsense" without resorting to vulgar euphemisms that refer to bovine fecal matter?

By suggesting that a law be passed, the editors of the *Times Union* aren't "asking" gun owners to do something; they are insisting that gun owners be required to jump through yet another hoop in order to exercise a constitutionally-protected civil right. Were this any other civil right – say freedom of the press or freedom of speech – such editorials would never be published, as the proposition would be laughed or shouted indignantly out of the newsroom.

Arguing that a gun owner's constitutional right to bear arms be subject to the approval of four other citizens is utterly ridiculous. Name another civil right that can only be exercised after a popular vote.

The newspaper argues – as others have – that it should be entirely acceptable that someone submit an application that can be approved or denied by a bureaucracy, just to exercise a civil right that should never be subject to that kind of limitation. This is precisely the kind of impairment that the Founders feared when they specified in the Second Amendment that the right to keep and bear arms "shall not be infringed."

With each sensational crime comes the almost obligatory call from newspaper editorialists and syndicated pundits that the United States must "tighten up" its gun laws.

The monumental disingenuousness of such blather defies the very principle of reason that such editorialists contend is at the foundation of their plea.

Criminals, by their very nature, do not obey laws, so they are certainly not going to obey yet one more law that makes it more difficult for the honest citizen to arm himself or herself. To suggest otherwise is to engage in foolishness, with an emphasis on "fool."

Yet the drumbeat for "tighter laws" on gun ownership has become a mantra of the Left. What they are really after are laws that make it impossible for even the most honest citizen to maneuver in order to keep a firearm for any purpose. The goal of these media-based gun prohibitionists is disarmament, and the fact that they are too cowardly to admit it does not mean the threat is any less genuine.

It is not merely disappointing but discouraging that so many in the press were quick to accept the arguments from the gun prohibitionist lobby following the Supreme Court's ruling in *District of Columbia v. Dick Anthony Heller* that the high court's majority had somehow re-written 200 years of judicial history.

They accepted, without challenge, statements like the one released by Kristen Rand, legislative director of the vehemently anti-gun Violence Policy Center in which she asserted that the court ruling ignored historic fact.

"Today's opinion," Rand argued, "turns legal logic and common sense on its head."

"In its ruling," she continued emotionally, "the Court has ignored our nation's history of mass shootings, assassinations, and unparalleled gun violence. It has instead accepted an abstract academic argument with dangerous real-world results for residents of the District of Columbia."

There was no skeptical analysis of the statement issued by the Brady Campaign to Prevent Gun Violence that was also grounded in emotionalism rather than fact.

"Our weak gun laws," said the Brady Campaign, "lead to tens of thousands of senseless gun deaths and injuries in this country. We must continue to fight for sensible gun laws to help protect you, your family, and your community."

But Justice Antonin Scalia's majority opinion, perhaps predicting such reactions from the prohibitionist lobby, offered a rebuttal to this very line of emotion-based rather than fact-based reasoning.

"We are aware of the problem of handgun violence in this country," the learned Justice wrote, "and we take seriously the concerns raised by the many *amici* who believe that prohibition of handgun ownership is a solution…Undoubtedly some think that the Second Amendment is outmoded in a society where our standing army is the pride of our Nation, where well-trained police forces provide personal security, and where gun violence is a serious problem. That is perhaps debatable, but what is not debatable is that it is not the role of this Court to pronounce the Second Amendment extinct."

The April 2009 "hit piece" on gun ownership by ABC's Diane Sawyer that aired as an hour-long segment of its "*20/20*" news magazine virtually demonizing the notion of having guns for personal protection is another manifestation of media bias. It is a pathetic display of arrogance and ignorance at the same time, as these advocates for tighter restrictions on one civil right seem to overlook the likelihood that once such restrictions against the right to have firearms become acceptable, government demagoguery will turn its attention to the First Amendment as a way to restrict, if not completely silence, criticism.

Blindly endorsing every increasingly restrictive gun control proposal, especially ones coming from the media-adored Obama administration or from the Far Left establishment politicians on Capitol Hill and in state legislatures, diminishes the credibility of the press, and weakens its ability to act as the "watchdog" on government that newspaper pioneers envisioned many generations ago.

A once energetic and skeptical press has been replaced by an activist cadre of reporters and editors who see themselves as among the ranks of self-appointed "progressives" (the term "liberal" is now shunned by the Left), rather than as a check, and perhaps even a balance, to a political philosophy that has taken on the trappings of a religious movement. These people have become no less the *jihadists* than the fanatics who cheered at the destruction of the World Trade Center; disagree with their philosophy and they make every effort to destroy you.

Ask Alaska Gov. Sarah Palin. Ask Samuel Joseph Wurzelbacher, also known as "Joe the Plumber."

Better yet, ask co-author Alan Gottlieb, who was targeted by some of the most vile hate mail one might imagine following his appearance on MSNBC's *Hardball* program with substitute host David Schuster on April 6, 2009 mentioned earlier. During the segment, Schuster – revealing himself to be more interested in pandering hysteria than presenting a fair debate – repeatedly interrupted Gottlieb, accused him of defending Nazi imagery used in relationship to the Obama administration by Fox News' Glenn Beck, and essentially preventing him from speaking.

Following that appearance, Gottlieb received several e-mails, the more tame of which included these:

From "Chris A":

"Will you all be able to function without a bogey man to scare you? Fuck off you cowards."

From "RCarli":

"I just watched your interview on Hard Ball. You are one of the reason there are some may uniformed whites in America. Your politics of fear are a detriment to America and leave a lot to be desired. It was clear to me, during your interview, you couldn't cite a specific instance of fact for the vitriol you spewed against President Obama.

"America already has an affliction that cannot be easily overcome, ignorant whites who love to hate. People like you and the GOP has been using hate and fear for decades to push your agenda; however, nobody buying it anymore except the few bigots left in the GOP...

"You came across as a coward whose bravery is only realized with a gun and without the gun, you are a small empty man full of hate."

From "Mark W":

"Hypocrites, traitors and advocates for murder!!!! Why do you want to destroy the beloved country we have fought so hard to protect!!!!

"Next time send your spokes person to a Speech Therapist if you want to be taken seriously.

"You traitors! We the people of the United States will be watching you! Be careful what you wish for....you might just get it."

From "Todd V":

"I saw Mr. Gottlieb on MSNBC's Hardball and I'm horrified at the ignorance, dishonesty, and fear mongering on behalf of your organization. Mr.

Gottlieb full-on lied about President Obama, Secretary Clinton, and others…I don't know why you're so hell bent on people's rights to shoot others, but there's something sick going on, and my only solace is that the spiritual consequences of what you're doing will indeed be awful. Sadly, you're wrong about Pres. Obama--I only WISH he wanted to take away your guns--the country would be much safer and more civilized."

One cannot find much room for serious discussion or rational debate amid this sort of vitriol. Yet after a couple of generations of subtle and not-so-subtle media indoctrination, it is perhaps understandable that some people lose all self-control when discussing gun ownership rights. As we said in Chapter One, some individuals simply hate firearms and by default, the people who own them.

As a result, it is the rule rather than the exception for gun owners to be dismissed and marginalized by the press. Thus, when a new proposal is put forth, it is greeted rather than analyzed by the press, and the obligatory request for comment from firearms owners or organizations is all too often reduced to a single sentence in a story or a single soundbite during a broadcast piece.

And, yes, there are new proposals masked as efforts to stem an alleged flow of firearms to Mexican drug lords, or roadblocks to terrorists and mass killers, and barriers to the arming of right wing anti-government fanatics. Interestingly, a Department of Homeland Security (DHS) Assessment that was leaked to the public in early 2009 suggested that "rightwing extremists" include citizens opposed to new restrictions on firearms, and returning military veterans. We will discuss this document momentarily.

First, we look at the so-called "Inter-American Convention against the Illicit Manufacturing of and Trafficking in Firearms, Ammunition, Explosives, and other Related Materials." It was revived in the spring of 2009 by the Obama administration as part of a high-profile trek by President Obama, Secretary of State Hillary Clinton and others in the administration to Mexico City. This international treaty had been languishing in the U.S. Senate for several years since it had been signed by the Clinton administration but never ratified.

Resurrected and advertised as a measure to prevent Mexican drug criminals from getting guns from the United States, its first section would criminalize the tradition of reloading one's own ammunition.

Millions of American shooters reload their own cartridges for any number of reasons, including hunting, target shooting and competition.

This treaty would define such ammunition reloading as "illicit manufacturing" if it is done without a license "from a competent government authority." It would become a crime to make one's own ammunition without a government license, and whenever such a license is mandated, along with it come restrictions and intrusive government regulation. Ultimately, it leads to a system or at the very least an interpretation of such a statute as allowing for the denial or revocation of such a license.

Bad enough that this measure would be introduced in a piece of federal legislation, but the fact that it appears in the first Article of a proposed international treaty both alarms and enrages American gun owners who reload their own ammunition. It sends a signal that the architects of this treaty wish to erode constitutional protections for gun owners by controlling not their firearms, but their ammunition.

Article IV of this document requires participating nations to "adopt the necessary legislative or other measures to establish as criminal offenses under their domestic law the illicit manufacturing of and trafficking in firearms, ammunition, explosives, and other related materials." This would make reloading one's own ammunition without the necessary government license a crime, most likely a federal felony.

In short, gun owners see this as a serious back-door assault on their gun rights.

Which brings us back around to the DHS report, titled *"Rightwing Extremism: Current Economic and Political Climate Fueling Resurgence in Radicalization and Recruitment."* When it was released under Homeland Secretary Janet Napolitano, the former Arizona governor who established an anti-gun record by vetoing important gun rights legislation in the Grand Canyon State, America's conservatives, military veterans' groups and gun owners were insulted.

This document, apparently never intended for public consumption, essentially labeled as "rightwing extremists" anyone opposed to the passage of new restrictions on firearms, and returning military veterans who were "facing significant challenges reintegrating into their communities." It likened them to racists because it argued that "rightwing extremists have capitalized on the election of the first

African American president…to recruit new members (and) mobilize existing supporters…"

So angry were veterans' groups that they demanded, and got, something of an apology from Napolitano. But the half-hearted apology did not extend to other groups that this report smeared, and because of that, their concerns about attacks on gun rights and other civil rights were only intensified.

The document, in a footnote, noted that "Rightwing extremism in the United States can be broadly divided into those groups, movements, and adherents that are primarily hate-oriented (based on hatred of particular religious, racial or ethnic groups), and those that are mainly antigovernment, rejecting federal authority in favor of state or local authority, or rejecting government authority entirely. It may include groups and individuals that are dedicated to a single issue, such as opposition to abortion or immigration."

Conservatives, pro-life Christians, Libertarians and others, including gun owners, were incensed. The report also labeled as "rightwing extremists" people who are "antagonistic toward the new presidential administration and its perceived stance on a range of issues, including immigration and citizenship, the expansion of social programs to minorities, and restrictions on firearms ownership and use."

While offering what was essentially a "lip service" apology to veterans' groups, but none of the other social interest groups, Napolitano suggested that the report might have been better edited or written. She did not disavow its contents. Indeed, on more than one occasion, she stood by the report.

Viewed objectively, this DHS report is yet another indication that conservatives, and particularly gun owners, are being marginalized. Such an official viewpoint does not render the firearms community irrelevant, but it does tend to diminish their political influence and gun rights activists within that larger community view this development as a step in the process of erosion of their rights by ignoring their concerns to the point of insulting their lifestyle and their concerns about the future of gun ownership in a nation that has a tradition of gun ownership.

As noted in an essay under the title "Will America Be Safer Without Guns?" co-authored by gun rights authority David Kopel of the Independence Institute and Jarret Wollstein, a member of the board of directors of International Society for Individual Liberty, "America was born as an armed society. Guns are an integral part of our traditions and remain essential for the preservation of our safety and our liberty."

This essay was part of the Second Amendment Project by the Independence Institute.

Gun rights historians will quickly note that the campaign to restrict and ultimately prohibit firearms ownership by private citizens in the United States has been one of attrition rather than an all-out frontal assault to literally rip the Second Amendment from the Bill of Rights, as that would never pass public muster with any group other than the extreme Far Left, especially now that the Supreme Court has ruled that the amendment does protect an individual civil right.

That said, gun rights activists view with a particular jaundice such things as an international treaty that discusses anything having to do with firearms and ammunition, or a report prepared by a government they feel may be hostile to civil liberties, that suggests citizens who believe in smaller government and adherence to a strict constitutional philosophy are somehow on the fringe, and therefore should have no relevance.

Once an individual or a social class becomes irrelevant, it becomes easier for society – a Utopian society as envisioned by those striving to create it – to disregard their concerns and their civil rights. Ask the Jews living in pre-Holocaust Germany.

Historically, no matter how restrictive a gun law happens to be, gun prohibitionists and their press cheerleaders never seem satisfied. It can be demonstrated time and again that with every sensational crime involving firearms, a new round of calls for "tighter gun laws" will be issued, as if one more law will provide the panacea for which the prohibitionists are looking.

Ultimately is becomes clear that what they want is the "perfect" society on their terms, by their definition. It would be a society without challenge and without risk, where rugged individualism may be an unpleasant memory, and self-determination a trait to be avoided so as to not upset an orderly community.

To such Utopians, the firearm is not merely a potentially lethal weapon, but a symbol of the kind of society they wish to replace.

The assault on weapons is really an assault on all individual rights, because it is an attack on individuality, which is a uniquely American trait. Perhaps it is something that has developed in the gene pool over generations that can be traced back to the earliest settlers who had to carve some semblance of civilization out of a wilderness. There was no police force to protect them from trouble, be it marauding Indian bands or highwaymen. They took care of that themselves.

There was no federal government – indeed, no government at all in most cases – to provide food and housing. If hard times set in, the government would not come along and offer a handout. One picked his own land, cleared it and planted his crops, and built a life as best as he could.

In the event of war, and there were a couple of bad ones early on – the French and Indian War and the Revolution that established this nation – no army would be dispatched to protect the frontier. That was up the frontiersmen who formed militias, kept their own long rifles or muskets, powder and ball at the ready. As the battles of Concord and Lexington clearly demonstrated, God help the fool who tried to take away those arms, as troops under General Thomas Gage's command learned at a dear price on the road back to Boston in April 1775.

As Koppel and Wollstein noted, "Regardless of the penalties for disobedience, millions of Americans will not peacefully surrender their guns. Many normally honest and law-abiding citizens will lie, evade, and perhaps kill to defend their rights."

Quoting George Mason University Prof.Walter Williams, a nationally-syndicated newspaper columnist, the authors noted that he had editorialized, "You'll know Williams is disarmed when Williams is dead."

Their assertion is simple, and blunt: "The bitter irony of gun prohibition is that laws intended to make America safe could spark the bloodiest violence in our history. Gun prohibition is not good for you, your family, or America."

This is not the ranting of some Internet fanatic, but two intellectual individuals who see the genuine danger of a unilateral civilian disarmament effort in the United States. One should not be so self-delusional so as to conclude that American gun owners will all meekly stand in line as did Australian and British gun owners to deposit their cherished firearms for destruction in some central collection site, keeping only photographs and fond memories of those rifles, pistols and shotguns as reminders of a tradition that once was, but is no more.

Defiant gun owners adhering to that tradition, regardless how anachronistic it is portrayed by the press and gun prohibitionists, will resist. What course that resistance will take is open to conjecture, be it purely political and legal in nature, or as Kopel and Wollstein suggest, violent.

Whether the threat or fear of violent resistance to an outright gun ban and confiscation, with an accompanying pattern of retribution against its architects, is what keeps the prohibitionists in check is debatable. What is not debatable, however, (to paraphrase Justice Scalia) is that the prohibitionist movement would require complete submission and compliance from a population to which those concepts are foreign and not the least bit abhorrent.

For the Utopian model to succeed, if one can call such a scenario a "success," individualism would not be acceptable and resistance would not be tolerated.

At least some gun rights activists suggest that possibly the greatest drawback to creating the Utopian society is that its inhabitants may one day be nothing more than the Eloi of H.G. Wells' *The Time Machine*. They are described in a Wikipedia entry about the famous novel as a "spoiled, attractive group, living a banal life of ease on the surface of the earth." It is up to the reader to decide whether there is anything familiar in that description as it applies to the current generation of "progressives."

Yet, as one gets deeper into the story, the idyllic lifestyle of the Eloi is a horrible façade hiding a grisly reality, for it is revealed that the Eloi are pampered and provided for by a subhuman species called the Morlocks, who attend to their needs only because they are *food*.

It is not that we, as a society, could one day degenerate into two species, one cannibal and the other a mere source of protein, but the metaphor of the Eloi and Morlock symbolizes the kind of society we could become where the masses come to depend upon a central government for all of their needs, because they lack the skills, and the tools, to resist.

In the firearms community, those promoting the Utopian dream and those eager to live in such an environment are often described as "sheep." They are compared to the grazing animal for many reasons, but primarily – in allegorical terms – it is because they depend upon shepherds for protection from the wolves.

America is at a crossroads, and we must decide whether we are a nation of men or a nation of sheep.

Gun owners have already made that decision, and have concluded that in a world of sheep, they are not part of the flock.

Demonization
and Hope

Demonizing one's opponents is a political strategy that has been around probably forever.

Democrats and liberals will rant about the "dirty Republicans" and stupid conservatives, and vice versa. Conservatives will point to the disastrous effects that liberalism have had on inner cities, education, health care and any number of other subjects, and remark that "If this is 'progress,' we don't need any more of it."

This is part of the political give and take, and there are times when it can get pretty rough-and-tumble, but when conducted between competing philosophies, the result typically finds the majority coming down somewhere in the middle on every fairly-debated issue.

But what happens when government intervenes? What becomes of a debate when it becomes official government policy to demonize one side or the other, laying blame for all manner of trouble at the feet of a particular interest group?

When we set out to write this book, it was long before the Obama administration began capitalizing (there is no better word, actually!) on the bloody violent drug war going on in Northern Mexico, with various officials including anti-gun Attorney General Eric Holder, Secretary of State Hillary Rodham Clinton and Homeland Security Secretary Janet Napolitano among others strongly attempting to blame the violence on American gun owners, manufacturers and dealers, and American gun shows.

Not coincidentally, the release of a report by the Brady Center to Prevent Gun Violence titled *Exporting Gun Violence: How Our Weak Gun Laws Arm Criminals in Mexico and America* in March 2009, it was something of an off-shoot of a campaign against what gun prohibitionists have dubbed "The Iron Pipeline," which is blamed for funneling firearms illegally from various states into New York, Chicago and other areas governed by strict gun laws.

The timing of the report and the visits to Mexico by Obama administration officials, none of whom skipped an opportunity to blame Mexican violence on American guns, is beyond the level of merely suspicious. The gun rights community campaigned strenuously against the November 2008 election of Barack Obama and within months it was obvious that they had good reason to be apprehensive about his ascension to the Oval Office.

Erroneous tales about how 90 percent of the guns being used in Mexico have been traced to United States origins were so often repeated that they became accepted fact. Propagandist Josef Goebbels would have been proud. To its discredit, the American press blindly repeated the statistic without checking the facts.

In a surprising opinion piece by Republican Utah Senator Orrin G. Hatch that appeared in the *Main Street Business Journal* in April 2009 – remarkable because members of Congress rarely weigh in on the subject of gun control with specific attention to such a detail – Hatch blistered the press for repeating the 90 percent canard, and he set the record straight.

"For example, a recent *Washington Post* story reprinted in the (Salt Lake) *Tribune* cited a statistic that 90 percent of guns seized from criminals in Mexico that are submitted for tracing can be linked to the U.S.," Hatch wrote. "This statistic has been cited by many, including the Secretary of State and Attorney General, who argue that the vast majority of guns confiscated from drug traffickers and other criminals in Mexico came from the U.S. This has become a major justification advanced by anti-gun activists and politicians to justify stricter gun control laws. However, those numbers are extremely misleading as the vast majority of guns confiscated in by Mexican law enforcement cannot be traced. In fact, only about 17 percent of the total guns confiscated in Mexico have been traced to the U.S."

"Worse than uncritically citing this statistic without context," Hatch continued, "this article blamed the 'western ethos' of support for the Second Amendment for problems related to gun smuggling and violence on the border between U.S. and Mexico. It stated unabashedly that an accused gun smuggler was released simply because the U.S. is a 'gun country.' What was not mentioned was the fact that the defendant was released because the judge found that the prosecutors had not provided sufficient evidence to support their charges. Apparently, that whole 'innocent until proven guilty' thing is just another relic of the Wild West mentality."

Predictably, the Hatch article did not receive as widespread attention as it perhaps deserved, because it went against the grain of what the press had come to accept as true (though it was verifiably false), and in the process, it criticized two newspapers in the process.

During the first months of 2009, the Department of Homeland Security seemed to be driven to marginalize and demonize so-called "extremist" movements and individuals, as noted in Chapter Twelve. Like the Missouri document, this "report" was never intended to be viewed by the general public, only law enforcement agencies. On the heels of its release of a document aimed at identifying "rightwing extremists," DHS also issued a "Domestic Extremism Lexicon" that seemed to attack just about everyone's favorite movement, from animal rights to black separatists to the tax resistance movement. Significantly absent by specification were gun rights or Second Amendment activists and Islamic or Muslim groups. The militia movement was mentioned, and so were Mexican separatism, the Patriot movement and something called "racial Nordic mysticism."

Why were not gun rights and Second Amendment groups included? Quite possibly the reaction to DHS' earlier document suggesting that "rightwing extremism" attracted such a negative reaction that they didn't dare.

Or, it might be that the authors figured they had it covered. The "militia movement" was noted to include members who "oppose most federal and state laws, regulations, and authority (particularly firearms laws and regulations)…" Thus, it could be argued, gun owners were linked to the militia movement by a subliminal suggestion that people opposed to firearms laws and regulations – regardless how onerous they might be – might somehow be part of, or at least sympathetic to, the militia movement.

After the 2008 Supreme Court ruling on the Second Amendment, there is not going to be a blatant frontal attack on gun rights. The Gun Control Act of 1968 and the 1994 Clinton ban on so-called "assault weapons" were the most energetic efforts to curb gun rights. More often these legislative attacks are designed to produce subtle erosion of the right to keep and bear arms.

However, that does not appear to be blunting the efforts of anti-gun bureaucracies, especially those with the ability to influence local and state law enforcement efforts under the guise of homeland security, to view gun rights activists and organizations with more scrutiny.

Considering the frenzy buying of firearms and ammunition following the 2008 national election that gave control of both the White House and Congress to the Left, any effort to rush forward with a renewal of the semi-auto ban was blunted, but not entirely stopped.

Where they may have initially had hopes that the Obama administration would open the floodgates for a wave of gun prohibitionist legislation, public opinion polls on gun rights tended to cool those jets.

Two significant polls were announced in spring 2009, one from CNN and the other a joint poll conducted for NBC and the *Wall Street Journal*. The CNN poll revealed that 46 percent of Americans believe existing gun laws are adequate and another 15 percent believe gun laws should be relaxed. Only 39 percent of the respondents support the enactment of stricter gun laws.

The NBC/WSJ poll found that support for renewed restrictions on so-called "assault weapons" had dropped significantly over the previous 18 years, from 75 percent in 1991 to 53 percent in 2009. It could hardly have been a coincidence that many Americans who had never previously owned a semi-auto rifle had bought one of those guns, perhaps out of fear that Obama's administration would ban them, and maybe because of the economic uncertainty sweeping the nation since the new president took office.

The battle over gun rights occasionally takes a bizarre and ironic turn, and that certainly defines the furor that erupted in May

2009 when Barack Obama released his 2010 budget proposal that sought to protect sensitive gun trace data, maintained by the Bureau of Alcohol, Tobacco, Firearms and Explosives. When he ran for office, Obama had essentially promised to repeal a statute, called the "Tiahrt Amendment" after its original sponsor, Rep. Todd Tiahrt, a Kansas Republican, that prevents big city mayors and gun control lobbyists from accessing that trace data for use in harassment lawsuits against the firearms industry.

Showing how rabid the anti-gun lobby can be even against its own "Chosen One" candidate, the Brady Campaign to Prevent Gun Violence and the Freedom States Alliance launched tirades against Obama, who suddenly became a pariah rather than "The Messiah." Both groups have wanted to strip the Tiahrt language from federal statute since it was passed.

Paul Helmke, president of the Brady Campaign, lamented, "This policy has allowed guns to remain in the hands of hundreds of criminals."

The anti-gun *Philadelphia Inquirer* wrote a scathing editorial suggesting that Obama had caved to the gun lobby, calling his retention of the Tiahrt language – at the urging of the BATF and Fraternal Order of Police, not the firearms community – "a death sentence for the hundreds of people slain each year by gunfire."

The rhetoric became worse when Obama signed into law a statute allowing loaded guns in national parks. Gun prohibitionists had filed a lawsuit to block implementation of a new parks rule, adopted in the waning days of the Bush administration, and when a federal judge upheld their complaint, the Obama Justice Department declined to appeal.

But Oklahoma Sen. Tom Coburn, a Republican, added language to – of all things – a credit card reform bill – and got the "rule" passed as a federal statute. This provided another opportunity for anti-gunners to protest that opening up the parks to armed citizens would endanger other visitors and lead to increased poaching. The point of the exercise was to smear gun owners as generally careless types who could not be trusted with firearms inside parks, even if they are trusted *outside* of the parks.

Barack Obama's first choice nominee to the U.S. Supreme Court to succeed retiring Justice David Souter in the spring of 2009 was federal appeals court Judge Sonia Sotomayor, a liberal's liberal. Gun rights activists and others immediately contested the nomination on various grounds. For the firearms community, Sotomayor's nomination sounded alarms because she was part of a three-judge Second District appeals court panel that ruled in late January 2009 that the Second Amendment was not incorporated under the Fourteenth Amendment to limit state and local governments from implementing broad gun restrictions.

In a 2004 opinion from a court panel on which Sotomayor served, the court held that owning a gun is not a fundamental right.

Supreme Court nominees can be counted upon to reflect the philosophy of the president making the nomination. Likewise, the individuals that the president nominates to open seats on federal circuit and district courts also earn their lifetime appointments in large part because their philosophy and their rulings have put them "on the radar screen."

Obama's presidency may not accomplish a frontal legislative assault on the Second Amendment, but in the long run, it will be how the right to keep and bear arms fares in the courts that really determines how broad or how restrictive the right will be enjoyed. This may become Barack Obama's legacy, how he stacked the federal courts with philosophical soul mates.

Many of the vacancies on the federal bench were unfilled during the final two years of George Bush's term because Democrats blocked the nominations. That left lots of seats open to be filled by the Obama White House, which started selecting nominees from the Left.

This is how the assault on weapons takes on its most formidable and insidious form. As a Second Circuit judge, Sotomayor told an audience in California that the appeals court is "where policy is made." That is a dangerous philosophy toward liberty, as it establishes the courts as a quasi-legislative body, and opens the gates for judicial activism. The *Washington Times* editorialized, "But judicial activism is no joke. It undermines the Constitution and substitutes judicial whim for democratic decision-making. Unelected judges answerable to no one but themselves and serving for life, can all too easily become dangerous oligarchs."

It has long been feared that the end of the United States as we know it and grew up with it will not happen in a rush, but by slow erosion, the incremental, almost unnoticeable, loss of civil rights. By the time we, as a nation, realize that rights have been lost or surrendered, it will be too late to do anything about it.

Contrarily, we have seen in the past couple of years, an affirmation that rights still exist, particularly gun rights. The Supreme Court struck down a gun ban on the grounds that it violated the Second Amendment, and in the process affirmed that the amendment protects an individual civil right. The Ninth Circuit Court ruled that the Second Amendment is incorporated to limit what state and local governments can do in regulating the right to keep and bear arms. As this book was written, the Second Amendment Foundation and National Rifle Association were pursuing several lawsuits aimed at striking down some of those local laws.

So, while there is a continued campaign of demonization against guns and the people who own them, efforts to restrict gun ownership in recent years have been unable to gain traction. Gun prohibitionists will continue with their irrational fear and hatred of guns, attempting to translate their personal prejudices into statute.

And gun owners will continue to fight, in the courts, in the arena of public opinion, and at the ballot box. An assault on gun rights is an assault on all civil rights, a proposition which may be difficult for some people to grasp. But gun owners know that when a government becomes so powerful and invasive that it can diminish one right – indeed, a right to bear arms in order to resist tyranny – then that government can just as easily move to curtail other rights because by then, the citizens will have lost the means to resist.

For this nation, that must not happen. We cannot allow it to happen.